Seeing Through the Cracks

A True Story

ELAINE USKOSKI

Copyright © 2018 by Elaine Uskoski
All rights reserved. This book or any portion thereof may not be reproduced or used in any manner whatsoever without the express written permission of the publisher except for the use of brief quotations in a book review.

First Printing, 2018

ISBN: 9781719978149

DEDICATION

I dedicate this book, with heartfelt gratitude, to my amazing tribe of girlfriends. You save my life every day!

*Cathy
All the best in the journey!*

ACKNOWLEDGMENTS

Thank you to my family and friends who supported me through this story's journey, as well as the writing process.

Thank you to my two editors, Harry Posner and Winifred Mellor-Hay, and my two beta readers, Erin Woodley and Marsha Michaels.

And thank you to my son, Jake for allowing me to share his personal struggle to help create awareness.

Prologue

They say that parenthood doesn't come from any how-to books, but I believe this to be untrue. Our own mothers and fathers write the book on parenting; their behaviours, both lousy and favourable, are modeled for us from birth. Some write a fairy tale, full of wholesomeness and effervescent adventures, while others create a mediocre tale of discipline, values, and ordinary experiences. And then there are those who write a horror story of atrocity, dysfunction, and cruelty. Of course, as their children, we not only read the book, we must fully participate in the tale. And then we must decide, as adults, and as parents, whether we want to carbon copy their version, alter some of the chapters, or perhaps even tear up the pages and create our own new book. Every child is faced with this same challenge. I was no exception.

In my youth, I didn't believe that motherhood would be a role I would take on. Like so many other young women in their early twenties, I was enjoying a time of freedom from responsibility other than for myself, my job, and my friendships. It was the eighties, a time of big hair, shoulder pads, blue eyeshadow, leg warmers, new wave, pop, and punk rock music. Having the freedom to play, drink, dance, laugh, and imbibe in complete and utter silliness was paramount in my life.

I came from a childhood home where oppression and control was the norm. My parents were very young and ill-equipped for the responsibility of parenting. My father was often absent, leaving my mother to parent alone. He was an alcoholic, who when he was at home, raged and spewed his anger upon his wife and his children. Both of my parents were never afraid to use physical force to create fear and obedience amongst my brothers and I. I didn't dare to challenge them, and while growing up I worked hard to get good grades and help with house chores and tried to keep a low profile. I felt terrified much of the time. My parents were writing the book on parenting in front of my eyes, and it was a horror story if ever there was one.

Once I became an adult and was living on my own, released from the shackles of my parents' domination, my behaviour became unrestrained. I became the "party girl" and having unbridled fun was at the top of my priority list. I didn't want anything to do with the book my parents had written for me. I wanted to toss it aside and run as fast as possible. We can never give up our desire to belong though, not entirely, and so I soon found myself in the arms of a local man, in love, and soon married. He was everything I thought I was lacking with my family; he wanted to be with me, he encouraged me, he loved me in return.

Life is unpredictable though. Like the reader who does not know what will happen in the next chapter, I was unprepared for what lay before me. Shortly into my new marriage, my baby brother was found dead at the bottom of a lake, the result of an accidental drowning, at the tender age of twenty. I was devastated by the loss. Shock, anger, and mourning colonized my being. Ahead of me was the immense task of learning to live each day, without my adored younger sibling. We had been close as children and still as adults, even moving across the street to be near one another. The thought of continuing life without my brother was unbearable at times. My friends had little understanding of my intense pain; even I had difficulty processing it. I slept more and felt a sense of heaviness and fatigue in performing daily tasks. My parents were numb in their loss and wanted me to provide them strength I was barely capable of giving. My eldest brother had moved thousands of miles from home and made a new life for himself. My remaining brother was so damaged by the cruelty of my parents that he was understandably emotionally-unavailable. And my husband, presumed love of my life at the time, maintained a sweep-it-under-the-rug philosophy of life, which left me feeling more isolated in my grief. He didn't talk about my loss with me, and I felt strongly that the overall expectation of me was to just get on with things. This was impossible. I was just not able to push down and lock away my enormous grief. I needed to talk about my loss and express my feelings, to be heard and recognized that I was hurting.

Soon after the loss of my brother I walked away from my constraining marriage. I realized I couldn't live with someone who would never be there to support me fully in my pain. This was my childhood all over again; the book of ugly parenting had returned. When I look back now, I know that part of leaving the marriage was me running from myself and my deep despair over the loss of my brother. I felt suffocated living within the confines of our childhood memories, every crevice of our hometown a reminder of my brother's presence, and an even more painful memorial of what could have been, what would never be again. I packed up and moved to the city and created a new life for myself, one of self-discovery through new friendships, fresh neighbourhoods, and an enormous hunger to burn away my grief, making it no longer recognizable, a mere smear of cheerless emotion. I grieved. I cried. I screamed. And when the emotional pain was too much, I partied, clubbing with friends, drinking and dancing, dissolving my angry and wounded emotions inside a hazy blur.

It was in this time, though, that I realized I could not just flee from my emotional wounds. The memories in my mind and the trauma they contained could not be escaped. It was not like my parents or my marriage; I could not simply walk out the door of my own emotions. I had to heal and prepare myself for the future. This was a defining moment for me and is where I would draw the strength later in life to hold the pen that wrote my own book on parenting.

I would get that opportunity to begin writing in my late twenties, when I met a wonderful man with a loving heart and an enormous capacity to give. He showed me true love, and my new approach on life led me to want to heal my emotional wounds of the past, and create a new life, including marriage and children.

Just three months beyond my thirtieth birthday, I gave birth to a baby boy, and my life would change dramatically, shedding my former self and morphing into something unrecognizable. Four years later, I was delighted to have a second son, a sibling for his big brother. My beautiful little family was now complete. Despite my own upbringing I now realized that I possessed a maternal depth I had assumed was unreachable. I felt I could write my own book, a more compassionate and nurturing story than my parents had created.

Of course, there were moments in my parenting that brought forward ugly memories of my own childhood. An inconsolable and demanding baby can raise one's blood pressure to the point of wanting to explode. Moments like these brought an opportunity for awareness of what I wanted and didn't want to create as a parent. Every day I made the conscious choice that I would mother from a gentler and healthier perspective than my own mother and father had. It was important for me to now create a footprint that would serve to be a great example, a story of good parenting for the next generation. I prepared to roll up my sleeves and take on the challenge. I would do whatever I could to provide a home that would feel safe and secure and be filled with massive amounts of love and joy.

It was obviously not easy to do. I made many mistakes along the way; I screamed, and I cried in agony, I laughed, and I soared in pleasure, but I stayed true to my goal. My intentions always came from a well-meaning place. I worked supremely hard, and as a parent, I am still a work-in-progress. Now, more than ever, I understand the tools it takes, the support it requires, and the perseverance and determination needed to make it work well. There is no cookie cutter set of rules or guidelines that work for every family, no universal text. From infancy to toddler, from youngster to teenager, each child is unique, and with that comes the opportunity for my own growth and adaptability, as well as theirs. I understand the challenges in the many phases of fostering a new generation and that even as adults, my sons still require my support and guidance. I keep an open mind, am willing to learn and adjust my approach, as required and I am constantly aware that my undivided attention to this role must meet a higher standard than the one I was modelled. This is the promise I made to myself and my children since embarking on this journey.

Now that I am writing my own story on parenting, I look back at the one my parents created for me to follow. I think about where it must have come from, and the tales I have gathered over the years from them are not pleasant. They also came from a history of dominance, and atrocious methods of parenting. Knowing what I do now, I hold no animosity for their behaviour. I understand that they made their choice as parents. They chose to copy the old book on parenting, perhaps because they lacked the tools, support or creativity to deviate. It was from this environment though, and my other experiences throughout life, that I drew the strength to break away from their path. I wrote my own book on parenting, and while it isn't finished, I hope it at least inspires my children to continue to build on the foundation I have created, thus far.

Chapter 1

It is late August 2013. My husband and I are moving our youngest son, Jake, into his dorm room at Guelph University, in a gorgeously opulent stone building. Jake's new room inside the building is dark, with just one tiny window. It houses three bunk beds with desks and drawers underneath. From the outside the building seems like something out of Hogwarts School of Wizardry, but inside it is a mass of typical dormitory dwellings. It is exciting for us to launch our second and youngest son into the post-secondary education experience. Student volunteers meet and direct us, as they did with our firstborn son, Nick, when he embarked on his adventure. We quickly unpack Jake's belongings and help to set up his new space. The move is easy, and Jake seems pretty happy to start settling into this fresh venture. He is about to begin a program in Computer Science Software Engineering, which includes a co-op program. He will spend his first and second year completing courses in classrooms and lecture halls. He will then be required to take co-op positions with technology companies, as well acquire more courses throughout the following three years, including summers. Software engineering has been an interest of his from a very early age and it feels like he has been preparing for this day all his life.

Prior to leaving the house to set off for Guelph, Jake had taken me aside and assertively proclaimed:

"Mom, I just want you to know that I will no longer be living at home. I will now live in Guelph and your home will just be a place I visit."

That sure hurt. I felt I had just been warned to back off in my parenting role and took it that Jake was heading out the door and wanted to be treated as his own, individual grown up self who could manage without us. It seemed abrupt and almost mean to my ear. We had a close relationship. I certainly didn't want to be pushed away so precipitously, but I also took comfort in hearing that Jake believed he had a good handle on this next phase of his evolution. I brush it off, not wanting him to see any evidence of motherly anxiety. Just as I did with Nick, four years prior to this, I approached the university launch as a time to celebrate and be happy for my son rather than making it all about me. And I truly am happy; I knew Nick had looked forward, with great anticipation to attending university away from home. And from his tone I could only assume that Jake was also ready for this new adventure.

For the next few weeks I stay busy entertaining my mother who is visiting from Victoria, BC, so I have lots to distract me. I am determined that I will give Jake the space he needs. I try not to send text messages, hovering and inquiring as to how he is doing each day. I let Jake take the lead and show me how he wishes the communications to be streamed. His father is not a big communicator via phone, email, or text, preferring to do his visiting in person, so I recognize that the majority of conversations will be between Jake and I.

I hear very little from my son the first two weeks of classes, and I do miss his presence at home.

Well into the third week of school Jake calls to say he is suffering with nosebleeds. He doesn't want to see a strange new doctor, on his own, and asks if I can come and take care of it with him. I'm not overly concerned about a few nosebleeds, but I am happy to have the opportunity to see Jake. I drive to Guelph and take him to a walk-in clinic. The bleeding is diagnosed as irritation and a little inflammation, nothing serious, perhaps the result of the dry air in his dorm room. I purchase a medicinal gel from the pharmacy for the interior of his nose. We have coffee afterwards and I prompt a discussion about whether or not I have been giving Jake too much space. I express concern that perhaps he was feeling ignored and that this little medical issue is a cry for some attention. Jake assures me that I am giving him the "perfect" amount of space. I am relieved. I return him to the campus and we hug good-bye.

I leave for home with a sense of satisfaction about being a good mom and not burdening him with my mistrust and worry these past few weeks. Things are cool, and I tell myself that I am being progressive with my parenting, allowing just the right amount of distance between Jake and I. "Good for me," I think.

The following week, I take my mom to Guelph for a visit with Jake and to see his university campus. We also go to lunch together at a local restaurant. He seems very happy and says that classes are going great. He looks tired, though, and his hair is a tad greasy. My guess is he now has less time for regular grooming and perhaps is not getting enough good sleep with his busy school schedule. After all, weren't we all a little careless when we first left home? Nick didn't wash his bedding for the first few months when he moved out. But the more I think about Jake's appearance, as I return home, the more unsettled I feel.

Chapter 2

It's early October and Jake leaves campus to join us in Toronto for birthday celebrations for his dad. He then comes back to the house for the weekend, his first visit since starting university. He seems happy, and conversations about school are very upbeat.

The next weekend Jake turns eighteen; now officially, on paper, at least, he's an adult. He returns home for his birthday celebrations as well as Thanksgiving dinner. All still seems well. Jake tells us about all of the friends he has made on the first floor of his residence and how they hang out in the hallways with their laptops working on their school assignments and socializing. He bought himself a beanbag chair to take out to the hall and join the other students. This is encouraging, and I believe I have nothing to worry about. Jake's managing his first semester very well.

In early November Jake returns home again for grade 12 graduation commencement at his former secondary school. This is an especially sweet celebration as Jake had a setback in grade 9 and then made up for it by completing secondary school in just three years. We are feeling very proud and are happy to have a formal opportunity to celebrate. Jake didn't want to attend but relented when I expressed to him that the ceremony wasn't just something for him to celebrate; it was for his father and I, as well. His body is visibly shaky, and he seems edgy, nervous, and unfocused. I ask him about it once the ceremony is over.

He says, "I'm just really happy and excited. I realized as the graduation ceremony began that I really do have a lot to be proud of and am glad that you convinced me to come tonight." Those words warmed our hearts and our spirits, and we relaxed more into the evening. It was a tough journey arriving here, not just for Jake but also for our entire family, and we just wanted to bask in the momentary glory.

During the remainder of the first semester there continues to be very little communication from Jake. When there is, it's vague. This is the opposite experience that I had with Nick, who sent me messages regularly and kept me abreast of much of his first-year university experiences. I do miss this with Jake, and it bothers me that he doesn't want to share. He had tended to be more private in his adolescence, and I chalk it up to him just being a very different person than his brother. This is his way, and I work to accept it. I hear little from Jake until mid-December when the semester ends, and he leaves his residence to come home for Christmas. He and Nick then begin making plans to spend lots of time together. My vision of the holiday break is much different. Nick has been living in the city with his girlfriend's family and commuting to school, his last year of university. I anticipated that Jake and Nick would be home and the house filled with much joy and laughter, as has always been the case. But Nick hasn't seemed himself recently, and there's been a tension in the house when he is home.

I am taken off guard a few days later when Nick decides to confront me with a flurry of complaints, telling me that I am interfering too much in his life, and telling me to back off. It feels shocking and hurtful; it's just not like him to attack in such a way. I get defensive and then I'm called out for that. So, I start listening; it hurts to hear it, but if we are to work through it, I need to give it my full attention. Nick has been a fiercely independent individual, and I have worked hard to give him the room needed to grow, but clearly, he's telling me that more separation is required. I recall doing a similar thing to my own mother when I was a teenager, and her reaction was to tell me that there was no validity in anything that I was saying. It only served to drive us further apart. I didn't want that to happen with my son, so I take it all in, and I accept responsibility for much of it. I apologize to Nick. It is vital to our relationship that I see what needs to be acknowledged, what behaviour needs to shift. I assume this is a normal part of a child establishing more autonomy as a young adult, and that this distressing confrontation is necessary for Nick. Even though Nick is clearly angry and frustrated, he also seems to feel some sense of remorse. In the middle of one of his rants he stops to tell me that I'm a good mother and he's had a good childhood. He begins to cry. I can see that this speaking up is tough for him, and obviously it has been seething inside of him for some time. We're both left feeling frazzled and shaken. It feels like a tornado just blasted through the house, shaking up the environment and clearing space for change. We retreat to our private corners of the house and allow the dust to settle.

With Jake's lack of communication of late, I've been guessing at what my next move needs to be and how to approach these next steps of parenting. With Nick, I'm just being told in a flurry of passionate words. He is giving me detailed directions. I'm not sure which I prefer.

Chapter 3

My husband, Brian, and I knew early in our relationship that we wanted to have a family together. There was no question we would try to make this happen. And upon hearing that we were pregnant with our first child, we were filled with joy. We were finally going to create a family and begin a new chapter together. It was very exciting. I'd be lying if I didn't say that there was also a weighted sense of concern.

Neither of us was really confident that we were equipped to be parents. We were unsure that we had the tools to make it work and not screw it up. I would hazard a guess that this reaction is normal for most people. None of us embark on parenthood with complete confidence that it's going to be perfect, unless all of the romanticism presented around it in the film and literary industries has convinced us otherwise.

My entire nine months of gestation were challenging. I gained only eighteen pounds total, making my obstetrician unhappy, but not particularly distressed. Although my body's blood circulation was thriving and flowing, providing me a warm glow, my digestive system was anything but thrilled. Food was not my friend, and as the months continued and my belly grew, it became more difficult to find anything for breakfast and lunch that didn't force itself back up mere moments later. Thankfully, by evening, my digestion settled, and dinner, at least, would remain in my system. I was losing some of my own body fat, but the baby was flourishing inside, and neither of us was in any real danger of malnutrition. I was definitely not going to have to deal with any post-partum weight, and I still maintained a degree of health that carried me to full labour and delivery.

What attracted me to my husband were his kind eyes and his sense of humour, and the fact that he could talk about any subject with great interest and enthusiasm. I value his opinion and look for comfort in his knowledge. He never surrenders an opportunity to share his quick and sharp wit. He's a joker and loves to laugh, and so do I. And this is what got us through the hours of labour and delivery. He was quick to learn how to be the most helpful support during my pregnancy, labour, and delivery.

It's no accident that they call it labour; giving birth to a baby is extremely focused and hard work. Brian had me, the nurses, and the doctors in stitches, laughing throughout the big event and, believe me, his humour was a greatly-needed gift when things got really intense. And when our first-born son finally arrived we both openly sobbed with overwhelming delight.

Nicholas arrived as an early Christmas present, the second week of December. He was four days past his due date, and seemingly hungry to make up for lost time. And I do mean hungry; he was a demanding newborn, looking to feed every two hours, around the clock for the first several weeks. I became quite exhausted and much panicked about how I was going to manage this kind of care on so little rest. He was a beautiful baby, and I instantly fell madly in love. I wanted so badly to do this motherhood thing to the best of my ability. During my pregnancy I read every book I could get my hands on, and now I was searching for more answers, and asking questions of other moms I knew. But the pressure was colossal, and as time passed and my baby's needs became greater, I just began to feel inadequate.

Brian worked long hours and because of his career, as an aviation engineer, travelled often. My parents lived on the other side of the country, and Brian's parents were enjoying their retirement wintering in sunny Florida. Our home was in a rural area, separating our neighbours by our five-acre property. I was alone and lonely, and at times frustrated with myself. I wanted it all to be smooth and easy and it was anything but. No one can really prepare you for motherhood, and it can quickly become overwhelming. That's not to say that there weren't many moments of extreme happiness, but I soon realized that I was not equipped to do this, and that it would be a struggle. Frustration and anger were overriding my happiness, and this is not what I imagined myself feeling as a new mom. The dream was becoming a nightmare and I was losing control.

Just before Nicholas's first birthday, I booked an appointment with my family doctor, and through tears of shame and fear I confessed that if I didn't get some help I was afraid I would hurt my baby or my husband, or both. A good night's sleep had become a thing of the past, and my days were spent in a daze of fatigue, surrendering my own personal needs for that of my child's. I was diagnosed with Post-Partum Depression, and the doctor made arrangements for me to start seeing a counsellor. This action saved my life and provided me with the support and the eventual tools for me to manage motherhood in a healthier, more positive manner. I saw the therapist every week for a full year, and I did my homework. I learned to put up boundaries for myself and lower my own expectations; I learned to be more self-nurturing, and take the time to rest, as I needed it, during the day. I didn't have to be Super Mom. I needed to be more self-accepting and be satisfied with doing the best that I could. And things eventually started to get easier. I felt much happier.

But, there are still moments when that Super Mom cape needed to be worn to avert disasters.

Chapter 4

During Jake's Christmas university break, an ice storm hits our area, and we start losing water and power in our home. This carries on for days and the weather forecast provides no news of relief. We have a family vacation planned, but instead of leaving together on Christmas Day, Brian remains behind to take care of the house. He is afraid the pipes could freeze and then burst, and we are no closer to knowing when our electricity and power will resume. Nick, Jake, Nick's girlfriend, Myles, and I leave for a week in Huatulco, Mexico. Brian hopes to join us in a few days, if it's possible. I hope he will make it. I feel outnumbered by these three young adults, and Nick and I now feel like strangers since his recent outburst.

Very soon after we've landed and settled into the condo rental, I begin to feel tension around Jake. I also start to notice how closely he is tied to his computer and social media, as well as online video games. He resists spending time with us on the beach or in other activities. He stays up until early hours of the morning to play interactive games and communicate with his many online friends and sleeps late into the day. I notice that his personal grooming is sliding and he's much more irritable with me. He is pushing the envelope of independence, and I assume this is a normal part of early adulthood. I don't like it. I decide to tolerate it, but only as long as Jake is not rude or disrespectful. At this point he is just being stubborn. He points out that he didn't ask to go on a vacation, that it was Nick's idea to get away over the

Christmas break. He also reminds me that he doesn't like sitting out in the sun, and a beach holiday would never be his choice. I know this is true. Jake has always preferred winter to summer. He has very delicate skin and has suffered some painful burns, in the past. It is unfortunate that Brian, who needs a break, is remaining home, while Jake, who doesn't appreciate the trip, has been made to tag along. The situation with the ice storm back home has still not improved, and sadly, Brian misses the vacation with us. Jake's attitude doesn't destroy our holiday, and he does participate in some of the activities; he and Nick bond over video games and talk of Anime and other things they both love. There are moments of joy and laughter, but I still feel frustrated with Jake's attitude. Nick is actually behaving more amicably than I had anticipated, but there is still an underlying strain. Thankfully, I am fortunate enough to have some fun female company in Myles. And I can say that for the most part, it's a good trip and feels fantastic to be in a warmer climate.

We pack up and leave the condo on New Year's Day and get a taxi to the airport. We have a really long wait to get through the check-in line at the airport, and when it is at last our turn, we are told that there is an issue with the flight. We will now have to wait for a confirmation on seating and are given standby passes. This is not a good sign, there is not another flight for a full week, and we all start to ponder the idea of being stranded. We eventually work our way through the security check and are off to our gate to wait. There are many passengers at this small tropical gate's holding area, and it's suffocatingly humid. We have to stand while waiting. Passengers are eventually called to board, but we are still not presented with confirmed seats on the plane. I am starting to feel panicked. I know that flights can be oversold, and we can get bumped; this has happened to me before with flying. I find an airline employee to inquire about the flight load and am told to wait a little longer and that the situation is being sorted out. The more time that passes, the less assured I feel that we will get on. My sixth sense is telling me that this may not have a good outcome.

We eventually learn that there are only five seats remaining. There is a family of four and a single man waiting with us. We avoid making eye contact with the others; we've done the math; there are nine of us and only five available seats. And when I hear that the others are called to board the plane, I realize that all hope of flying home on that flight is lost to us. My heart sinks, I feel sick and my heart begins to race. This is a nightmare. I am responsible for getting the four of us home, and I have no idea how to fix this. We return to the airport check-in area and start to ask the airline reps questions. How will we return home? Are there other flights available on other airlines? Are there seats available with other charters? The terminal representatives are all so kind and helpful, and one man in particular takes pity on us, working very hard to come up with a plan. Every inquiry comes up empty; each flight is already full. Nick gets an internet connection on his cell phone and contacts Brian back at home to let him know what's happening, and to see if he has any suggestions. Brian sets to looking up flights online for us. We have several people working to find a solution now, but I cannot relax. Everything is a dead end. We are ultimately told that our best chance of returning to Toronto would be to go back to our hotel and then return to the airport the next day. We have a slim chance of getting a flight all together, on standby, but more likely we could get out of Huatulco one at a time over the next few days. This is madness; at that rate it could take up to a week before we're all home. My panic grows into alarm, and I relinquish all control of my emotions, bursting into shameful tears. I have lost control of the situation and have no answers, no solution. I have failed Nick, Jake and Myles.

Nick comes to comfort me; he remains calm, but he also feels a much bigger urgency to get home. He has his part-time job to return to, as well as school. This is his last year at university and in a few days, he begins his final semester. He doesn't want to be stranded for another week. He is determined to somehow make this work. He becomes the strength for our little group and he continues to look for solutions with his dad, over the Internet. We then learn from my husband that if we can get out of Huatulco and get to Mexico City, then we will have no trouble finding flights to Toronto from there. We begin asking the airport representative about flights to Mexico City, but this comes up empty, as well. I feel imprisoned and hopeless. Nick asks me if it's possible to rent a car and drive to Mexico City. He suggests that he and I could take turns driving. To rent a car and drive, one must be at least twenty-five years old. Nick is only twenty-two, so if we drive it would be on my shoulders. I'm not certain that I want to take on the task of driving in a strange place and at night. Nick insists that it won't matter, that it's Mexico, they won't care. He wants to help; he wants to drive. But I think it's a bad idea. I say no.

More time passes, and all flights have left the airport en route to their destinations; we now realize there is absolutely no chance of getting out of Huatulco tonight, or possibly for the next week. Nick is still insistent on the driving plan. I am desperate to get us home and consider this option, and I calculate what it would entail to make this work. The flight from Huatulco to Mexico City takes just one hour. I determine how long that might take to drive. I have flown to Montreal from Toronto and it is a one-hour flight; I have also driven from Toronto to Montreal and it is a five-hour journey. It is evening and if all goes well, we could arrive sometime after midnight, and then check into an airport hotel until morning. Logistically, it seems do-able. I finally relent but tell Nick that only I will do the driving; I'm not prepared to have my son drive illegally, possibly get caught and find himself in a criminal predicament in Mexico; that could be very dangerous and scary.

We speak with the kind gentleman who had been trying to get us a flight, and he goes in search of a rental vehicle for us. We are both surprised and delighted that he has remained well past his work shift to try to assist us in any way that he can. He is like an earth angel and we are grateful for his compassion and kindness. We heard so many stories before leaving on this trip about how threatening and corrupt the people of Mexico can be, but we experience the exact opposite with this man. It takes another hour and a rental car has been found for us. We are told that it is the last remaining car in the rental lot. I take this as a good sign and start to feel a sense of relief.

I fill out the required paperwork and concede to pay an excessive $500 for the car, agreeing to drop off the vehicle at the Mexico City airport before 10:00 a.m. the next day. I believe this will be easy given my calculations on the distance that we will travel. Nick is still insisting that he will take on some of the driving, but his intentions are revised rather quickly when I am handed the keys to the car and told that it is a standard transmission vehicle. Nick has only learned to drive an automatic. So, it is settled; I will do all of the driving. The responsibility of navigating myself and these three young adults is now mine. I cannot fear this journey. I have made a commitment and I have to follow through. They are counting on me, and I must put any trepidation behind me, and act as though I am thoroughly confident in my ability to manage this. But the truth is that I am scared to death. I can't think about what could happen, I can't think about my apprehensions. I tell myself that I can do this. Nick, Jake, and Myles are behind me and encouraging me, saying that it's a good plan. At 7:45 p.m. I send a quick text home to Brian, telling him the plan, and then turn off my phone before he tries to talk me out of it. I get behind the wheel of the car, take a deep breath, and set my mind on autopilot. I am now strong; I am now fiercely determined. We will get to Mexico City in the next five or six hours. I can do this.

Chapter 5

Before we set off, we are given a small hand drawn map from the representative at the car rental station. Nick offers to handle the map-reading for the trip. All four of us agree to remain awake in order to support me, the sole driver. Nick, Jake, and Myles will take turns sitting up front in the passenger seat and keep me company. We have no food with us and our last meal was breakfast. We decide that we will make a stop very soon for gas and food. We have not been given a full tank. Jake suggests that I should consider drinking some kind of super sweet and highly caffeinated beverage like Red Bull to help me to stay alert for the drive. I am a holistic health practitioner; I don't even drink caffeinated coffee. I don't know how my body would react to this, but I consider it for later.

Once we leave the city lights of Huatulco, it becomes quite dark on the highway. It is a narrow two-lane roadway that soon appears to be built around a mountain, and we are on the inside lane, hugging the skirt. We have no idea where the next gas stop might be; there are no signs directing this. But there are seemingly endless signs indicating the many sharp turns on the road. The car has six gears, but I am rarely able to get it into fourth gear before needing to gear down to navigate another turn. We quickly discern that the only other vehicles that travel these roads at night are large tour buses and transport trucks. They seem to have a much better handle at maneuvering the challenging course and move at a greater speed than I. I keep the window open for fresh, cool mountain air that will keep me alert and help me concentrate. My hands are kept busy, shifting the gears up and down as well as signaling my headlights from normal to high beam and back again, as I approach either an oncoming vehicle, a curve in the road, or both. My legs muscles are put to good use switching from clutch to brake to gas, and I feel grateful that I am not sitting still. The focus required, as well as the deliberate physical motion helps to keep me on guard. At no point can I take my eyes off of the road. This is unfamiliar territory and although I have driven along many dark countryside roads in my life, none have offered such treacherous conditions as this mountain road. I begin to think that we're insane for even attempting this, and then quickly push that thought away. I must just keep concentrating on driving.

After the first hour on the road we come upon a petrol station, where we can fill up the tank and purchase some snacks. All that we can muster up are M & M candy and potato chips, and I get myself a Red Bull. As I am maneuvering the vehicle to leave I discover that I can't get the reverse gear to work. Thankfully we can move around and leave the station without the use of reverse, but I will need to continue to be aware of this as we pull into future stops. This is just one more challenge now, of many.

The Red Bull tastes terrible, and after I swallow it, it burps back up in my throat as a sharp foaminess. It literally feels like I am putting poison in my body, but hot coffee or tea do not seem to be available, and the guys tell me those wouldn't have the kick I'll need to remain awake. I am now concerned that I won't be able to sleep once we reach a hotel. We eat up the candies and chips, satisfying our hunger for the moment. We drive on, really still unsure as to where exactly we are. We come to a tollbooth and are suddenly struck by the fact that we need Mexican pesos to pay. We start collecting what we each have left over from our vacation and pool it for future tolls. We leave the booth and there appears to be a second route that we can take. It doesn't seem to be indicated on our scratched out, primitive map. We decide to stick to the road we were already taking, unaware that it is the longer of the two routes.

The route appears to be taking us all the way around the mountain, up and down and through vacant, dark areas with seemingly no settled towns for several miles in between. And when we do prepare to enter an inhabited place, we must slow down for large speed bumps that are difficult to anticipate until we are almost upon them. Along the route, there are signs to watch out for fallen rocks, and for cows and donkeys. There are no cellular towers, our phones will not connect if we are in an emergency, we cannot update Brian, and we cannot even listen to the radio in the car. It is us against the world, and we entertain ourselves and each other with stories, jokes, word games, and complete silliness; we are all starting to feel punchy, likely the effects of a combination of adrenalin, mountain air and increased altitude.

We manage to get through several toll booths on what little pesos we have and continue to hope with each one that it is the last we will have to pass through. We require a number of stops for pee breaks, not always able to find an open gas station with available washrooms. We look for roadside shoulders in remote areas. None of us will leave the vehicle to urinate unless a second person is standing watch. It is eerily quiet and difficult to see what is beyond the next bend. Between the stimulants of the Red Bulls and the pressure we're under to continue moving forward, our bladders all seem to be on overdrive. As the night progresses and fill-up stations are closing we start finding what appear to be roadside shacks that sell refreshments. We continue to fill up on caffeine, chips and sweets, and hope that our money lasts us to the end. The trip is taking much longer than we anticipated, and it is now well past midnight.

We enter into the tightest bend so far, and it feels like a continuous circle that we never straighten out from. This must be a smaller part of the mountain that lets us wind around it so quickly. Suddenly, I see a boulder up ahead on the road...and a tour bus approaching us from behind it. I start doing mental math as I calculate the space. There isn't enough of it. We can't squeeze by, and we're running out of road to brake in.

I immediately begin to gear down, my breath catching in my chest as the terror seizes me. I'm braking as fast and as hard as possible, and I can see he is doing the same. Passengers must be getting tossed forwards in his vehicle as we all try to come to a screeching halt.

Then we both stop.

I somehow manage to move my whitened knuckles, giving a little flash of my headlights to the driver in appreciation, and in recognition of the fact that we're all not dead. We all sink back in our seats and exhale a massive sigh of relief. As I begin to drive forward and pass the bus and rock, I realize just how close that was, and how damn lucky we were. We just missed a bus, literally, and we're a bit giddy thanks to adrenaline combining with the knowledge that we're all still alive. But we're not out of the dark yet.

Chapter 6

It's 4:00 a.m. and we have been awake for more hours than I'd like to recall. I have been able to feel the fuzz growing on my teeth throughout the night, and I'm sick of Red Bull. We're more than done with this drive. So, when we enter into another stretch of highway, I think nothing of it at first. Then I notice the four large transport trucks coming towards us in the other lane. And the one at the back wants to pass the other three.

Very recent memories of the bus instantly spring to mind. Once again there's no time to stop, and no way to avoid a collision. My heart is pounding, everyone in the car has started yelling about the impending danger, my palms are sweaty, the panic is filling up the air, suffocating us as we brace for impact.

The passing truck finds a way to squeeze in closer to its buddies. I pull over as much as possible to the furthest side of the road. This will be close. This will be a few inches kind of close.

I can feel the wind sweep my hair as the transport passes, a cool breeze blasting by, the kiss of another death that could have been. And yet, here we all still are. We're now teetering on the edges of our own sanity. This trip has moved from dangerous to ludicrous in the blink of an eye. I'm not done yet though. Even with every ounce of my body groaning at me, begging me to just pull over and quit, I push onwards.

Morning begins rearing its head and we are now aware that we are going to witness sunrise in the mountains of Mexico. Thankfully we are now travelling west, and the sun comes up behind us. It would have been blinding to have it appear in my sightline while driving. It's actually exciting to experience the dawn and gives us something to direct our attention to. It also brings light for my driving, making the dark, ominous roads a thing of the past. This gives me hope. But we have been travelling for so long and have still not reached our destination that I worry we will not actually be able to return the rental car by 10:00 a.m. We are seeing signs now telling us the distance we still need to drive before reaching Mexico City, and it seems an arduous task. My body is running on fumes, with little or no nutrition or sleep. My legs and arms are sore. I'm hungry for food and water. And it is obvious that we will not be falling into a hotel bed when we finally arrive. We will need to check in for our flight home. This has already become an exceptionally long journey and it's not over yet.

We arrive at another tollbooth and are now completely out of pesos. We have no idea how we will get through. I have Canadian money in my purse and suggest that we offer it. The booth authorities refuse my ten-dollar bill and start yelling at me in Spanish and waving their arms for me to back up. I cannot back up; the car's gear doesn't work, and I do not know how to articulate this back to them. I can speak only a few words in Spanish at best, and I am scared and frustrated. My body begins to shake inside, the terror rising to my chest. Nick is now in the passenger seat beside me and sees that I am panicked. He begins to speak in Spanish to the two uniformed men. I am never more pleased that we encouraged Nick to study languages. He manages to interpret their directions and tells me that they are saying that they can only accept Mexican pesos or American dollars. This isn't helpful; I don't have any American funds with me. I see a dark image, in my mind, of the four of us being carried off to a Mexican prison, and I begin to feel the terror of defeat. And then from the back seat, Myles tells us that her mother had given her a $50 American bill to take on the trip and that she doesn't remember exchanging it for pesos during the vacation. What feels like five minutes is really just seconds, but Myles eventually retrieves that bill from the bottom of her purse. None of us can believe our fortune and all of us are relieved by her mom's financial gesture; never in a million years would she have known how desperately that money would be needed. It is another of the many miracles we have been witness to on this incredibly insane adventure.

We hand over the money to pay our toll, and fortunately we are given back the change in pesos; none of us were sure that would happen. We are now in the clear if there is another tollbooth to pass through before arriving at the airport. And our faith in humanity continues. We have been gifted so many opportunities to see that people are essentially good, despite the stories and warnings we have heard about Mexico. I do understand that there is criminal activity here; I am not that naïve, but we have somehow been guided and protected through this part of the world, unscathed by any of it. The airport representatives, the rental car staff, the gas and snack station attendants, the tollbooth operators, and the other drivers on the road have all shown us nothing but kindness. We have discovered many more earth angels. We have been blessed and I do not take it for granted. There are more miles to travel, and we start to feel more optimistic that everything will be fine.

We drive on. In the early morning hours, we start to see more signs of life, larger communities in the distance with their lights glowing. There is now more traffic, and it is no longer just transport trucks and buses. The morning commuters are on the road. We finally see signs pointing in the direction of the airport and are now following that route. It takes about thirty more minutes before we finally approach the airport. We are elated and relieved that we've accomplished our mission. We celebrate the journey and the fact that we are all still awake and have supported one another through this ordeal. I thank everyone for keeping me going, as the only driver. Jake rolls down the window in the back and sticks his head out, yelling and screeching with abandonment. He can't contain his joy, and we don't want him to. We all feel it, too.

As we pull into the airport parking lot, something doesn't feel quite right. It seems rather empty and quiet, not the usual hustle and bustle you'd expect from an airport, especially at this time of day. We don't see any car rental facilities, either. We park the car and walk inside, and it is unnervingly silent. We quickly learn from the lone person at the counter that this is the domestic municipal airport; we need the international one. Suddenly our jubilation is met with incredible disappointment. We cannot believe that after all the hours we've just travelled on unfamiliar and scary mountain roads, bone-weary and hungry, wrestling with terrifying road blocks and dangerous conditions, that it's only brought us to the wrong destination! Really?

It is 8:30 a.m., we have been driving, with great determination and courage for over thirteen hours, and instead of celebrating our success, we are left with the overwhelming task of building ourselves back up and digging in harder for that much longer.

It's just demoralizing.

The thought of getting back into that rental vehicle and driving yet more miles is frustrating, but we have no choice. We obviously still can't get home from here. On the positive side, Nick points out that he is now able to connect to the Internet on his cell phone, and we now have a Global Positioning System (GPS) to rely on. Our paper map shows us no details of the city's streets and/or highway that will lead us to Mexico City's major airport. At this point we need any help that we can get. We literally have just ninety minutes to arrive with the rental or we will have to pay more tariffs for the car.

It's a weekday morning and it is still rush hour. Traffic is much heavier, and we are instructed by the GPS to get back on a major highway. It is many lanes wide and bumper-to-bumper. And the route to the airport seems far more complicated than the trip through the mountains in darkness. By now, Jake has finally surrendered to his fatigue and is asleep; it is up to Nick, Myles, and I to sort out the remainder of this mission. Honestly, without the GPS I am certain that we would have never found the airport on our own. With 15 minutes on the clock, we finally pull into the parking lot. We've done it. We've arrived. It may have taken us ten more hours than expected, and two near heart attacks, but it's all over now.

Although we have arrived at our destination, and we're one step closer to getting home, we're all feeling so numb and bone weary it seems an anticlimactic end to our insane journey. We're in an airport, there are no boulders or fast-moving trucks to dodge, only bustling travelers searching for their gate number. We at last feel safe, and the only sign we're destined to fight our way to is the one that's marked washroom.

Once cleaned up, I dig through my bag for a sweater. I am feeling chilled. I long for a warm cup of tea and a hot meal. I've been awake for more than twenty-four hours and haven't eaten a full meal in almost as long. My stomach growls and my legs want to buckle under the weight of my fatigued body. The rest of the gang are all chiming in at how hungry they are, so we head straight for the nearest restaurant. As soon as we are all seated, we realize we have family members who will be anxious to hear from us. We all turn on our electronics and connect to the restaurant Wi-Fi. After hours of isolation from communication, it's a relief to know that in an instant we can re-connect. Myles sends a message home to her family so that they know that she is safe. I quickly run off an email to Brian, who is now at work, to say that we made it to Mexico City, and that we are safe. Before our server is at the table to take our orders, Brian has replied with the message that never in his life has he been so happy to see an email from me! He is so relieved that we have arrived unscathed. I am certain that he had many doubts. He tells me that he didn't sleep much through the night, worrying about our safety. He is proud of us for our efforts and perseverance and so comforted to know we're all okay. He has already checked the flight loads and knows that we will have seats on the Toronto-bound departure.

We have a feast of a meal, eating as though we haven't eaten in a week. We talk and marvel at what we've just come through. Myles cannot stop thanking me for taking over the wheel and safely getting us to this point. I believe that I have earned a new respect from these three young adults, like a badge of honour. And I am proud of myself. But I could have never done it without them, and I tell them how proud and grateful I am. We have just travelled for fourteen and a half hours, through the dark night, in the mountains, in unchartered territories, facing many scary challenges, and yet we are all still talking, even making jokes, and not fighting with one another. It is in the darkest moments that we see what we're made of, and we discover that we all have what it takes to move through a large-scale crisis. This is an amazing lesson in tenacity and endurance, as well as teamwork. We have a lot to feel proud about.

Mid-afternoon, we board the plane. We take our seats and prepare for take-off; and then it's lights out for all of us. There will be no hospitality service, drinks or meals for any of us; just sleep for the next few hours. It won't be enough to fully restore our bodies and minds, but it will sustain us enough to get us through the next step, the arrival in Toronto. We will need days to recover and feel somewhat normal again. But I don't believe that any of us will ever feel the same about ourselves again. I personally feel like I have just conquered Mount Everest. No excuses; I am fully capable and shall never be able to say that I can't. Nick, Jake, and Myles may not see the lesson immediately; but as their futures unfold they will hopefully see that anything truly is possible when you are determined.

We are greeted at the airport by a very happy Brian, and he packs us into our vehicle and gets us home. We have quite a tale to share with him, which we do during the forty-five-minute drive home. We've had quite a week and quite an expedition, and we are so happy that's it's now behind us that we don't even care we've left tropical beaches and hot temperatures to return to our cold, snowy, and yet very welcoming winter weather. There's no place like home!

Chapter 7

As a youngster, Nicholas showed signs of great intelligence and an appetency to learn very early on. It was as though he was always in a race to the finish line to be all grown up. He spoke in full sentences by the time he was just eighteen months old. At age two he demonstrated an impressive physical hand-eye co-ordination. He was active and social, had a voracious love for books and stories, and developed an early love for anything humorous. His sense of humour was not juvenile in nature; he advanced quickly past typical silliness and toilet talk, developing a great comprehension for mature witticism. He often seemed like a miniature version of a witty young man.

While he was still three years old, Nicholas entered Junior Kindergarten. It was a huge day for both of us, but it seemed we were not on the same page with how we each expected his first day of school would play out. I wanted to drive him to school for his send-off, while he wanted to take the school bus. I tried to tell him that the moms always drive their child to school on the very first day, but he was having nothing to do with this argument. We were outside of our house and I was taking his photograph when the big yellow school bus appeared at the end of our very long driveway. Nicholas spotted the bus, and without a moment's hesitation ran down the driveway, his backpack flying up and down, and then jumped onto the bus. I stood there, now pregnant with our second child and feeling very hormonal and felt deeply disappointed by this abrupt departure. This was not the scene I had imagined. I decided that I would get in my car, drive to the school, and surprise Nicholas when he arrived there. In my state of disenchantment, I had fooled myself into believing that this was exactly what he'd want.

The school was just a five-minute ride by car, but the bus needed to make many stops for school children, so I made it there in plenty of time. I stood with great anticipation, believing that this surprise would bring such delight to my little boy. The bus pulled up and the children disembarked, and suddenly there was Nicholas emerging before me. My smile couldn't have been bigger when I saw his little face. He spotted me immediately, walked straight up to me, looked me in the eye with such a serious expression and said, "You can't be here, mom." And then he walked on into the school with the rest of the children, leaving me feeling utterly deflated. In my moment of humiliation, I realized that he was not having any separation issues; it was me who couldn't let go, and I knew immediately that I had nothing to worry about. I needed to cut this invisible umbilical cord between us and give him this space to grow on his own. I had just had my first harsh lesson in his need for autonomy.

The birth of his baby brother, Jake, was one of great delight. Nicholas was nurturing and kind, and from the moment he was made a big brother, he took to his role with great responsibility. There were many times that I would say to him, "Let me be the parent," as he always wanted to be the one to lead the way, set the example, and take care, literally, of his brother's every need. The two of them bonded with intensity so unfamiliar to me that I often felt a mix of delight and bewilderment at their relationship. My own three brothers were constantly, as children, fighting with each other. This experience was also new to some of the other mothers. They would often comment on the tight relationship that these two brothers shared and about how Nick was such a nurturing soul. Their surprise and comments led me to realize just how special this alliance was.

Demonstrating his maturity and need for independence was a constant for Nicholas. In grade one, at our first parent-teacher interview, we were informed that our son was doing exceptionally well for a December-born child. The teacher went on to say that she had late-in-the-year birthday students that she cried for because they couldn't keep up, and Nicholas was definitely not one of them. This was a relief for me, especially now that I had a second child to care for, and another indication of that sense of urgency to move on that Nicholas possessed.

Soon we shortened his name to Nick, as Nicholas didn't seem quite grown up enough to fit. He played hockey, soccer, and tennis, and thrived in athletic activity; eventually tennis became the dominant sport and many hours were spent at the courts with practices, coaching, and competitive matches. Elementary school seemed a good fit for Nick; academic studies came with reasonable ease. His core French teacher approached me one day while I was volunteering in the school and expressed her delight at Nick's interest and comprehension in her class. I later spoke with Nick about this and he was pleased, telling me how much he loved learning French at school. He then bravely made the jump to enter middle school for grade six to participate in the Extended French program; a time when most of his classmates were remaining in the elementary school in our neighbourhood.

Evidence of Nick's fierce ambition to be independent appeared often, and from age eleven onwards he would often ask me to take him to the IKEA furniture store in the city, where he would promptly race to the showrooms, taking in every detail, and choosing the kitchen, living room and dining room combination that he liked most. He would then happily proclaim that this was how he envisioned his own apartment when he would become an adult.

At age fifteen and in grade ten, Nick took a school course in Spanish and absolutely loved both the teacher and the concept of learning another language. He applied to an exchange program and was accepted. We initially hosted a student from Spain in our home, but Spanish was not spoken during this time, as he was to learn to improve his English. There was a three-month gap between the student's return to Spain and Nick's three-month trip to Santander. Nick had mixed feelings while away. He loved the city and enjoyed his days at school, but he was uncomfortable with the exchange family's dynamics and lifestyle. He felt that the parents were too harsh with their children and their rules, and the fighting amongst them. He began to feel unhappy living amongst the chaos in their home. True to his independent and in-charge nature, Nick eventually requested a return to his family home in Canada a few weeks earlier than the expected date. His request was granted, and Nick flew home to the safety net of his family.

In that same year Nick decided that his love of tennis had grown to the point where he wanted to get his Instructor's Certificate and start teaching children who were learning the game. He worked hard on the course, and once his goal had been achieved, he got a part-time job at a tennis club. By sixteen Nick had a driver's license, something he'd dreamed of and could barely wait to get. He got a second-hand car to drive to school in grade twelve, abandoning the big yellow school bus. From that point on, he and his best pal, William, rode to school in his car. That same year he advanced his tennis teaching qualifications to Club Pro level one, completing this a year earlier than the course age minimum. He took on the responsibility of coaching children during summer tennis camps. He was driving, he was working and earning his own money, and he was well on his way to becoming self-sufficient.

Nick graduated from secondary school with ease, his favourite subjects being English, History, and Drama. He began to inject his gift of creativity into the writing of short stories and then a full teen novel. Upon finishing grade twelve he entered university, living in residence. His major was English, and he decided to add to that a minor degree in History.

Year one flowed seemingly with ease, and he somehow managed to continue working part-time with the tennis club while maintaining his academic studies. Second year brought a challenge with some health issues that became acute and serious. A lump was discovered in Nick's neck, which at first was thought to be a swollen gland. Over time, the lump didn't dissolve, as was expected, but instead grew in size. Nick began to feel fatigued, and then suffered with dizziness, and at times, experienced difficulty breathing and swallowing. A number of weeks passed by, during which time various specialists ran Nick through several tests but couldn't agree on a diagnosis. Before it became clear that the mass in his neck would need to be surgically removed, Nick was rushed to the hospital one early morning, after complaining to me of chest pain and having difficulty breathing. He was then diagnosed with and treated for pericarditis, an inflammation around the sack of his heart. You can imagine my terror when I thought my nineteen-year-old son was suffering from a heart attack. Although it was a relief to know it was just inflammation, it was another setback to be dealt with before the surgery could take place.

Nick had also questioned his choice of English major and had decided to switch over to Earth Sciences in second year. It was not an easy transition. And it became a challenge to keep Nick in university residence with all of his health complications. It was terrifying at times, and the hospital emergency room and doctor's offices became all too familiar. For weeks at a time he lived at home and I drove him to classes. We provided him with a tutor to help him to keep up. Nick eventually underwent surgery and made a full recovery. During this time, he missed several days of classes and fell further behind in his studies. As time went on it was clear that getting through the school year was a far greater challenge than he'd anticipated and changing over to science courses was perhaps not the right decision.

Year two was a do-over year, and at that time Nick dropped his French studies and moved to the campus closer to home, commuting for the remaining three years. He also returned to studying English and History. It wasn't easy for him to commute; winter driving was difficult at times. Living at home again was not ideal for the young man who proclaimed from an early age that he couldn't wait to get a place of his own. Nick assured me that his need to be out on his own wasn't for the wrong reasons, and that he felt he'd had a great childhood, but he was always excited about the idea of having his own place to live. University residence brought him close to that experience. And now that option was gone.

There were some tense moments in Nick's last year of university; he was tired of the commute, coaching and playing competitive tennis was starting to break down his body, he had a girlfriend now in his life, and his time was divided between his relationship, school, and work. And then there was the nagging disappointment at still having to live with his parents. Nick started to stay in the city with his girlfriend's family, and we saw much less of him. When he was around he was withdrawn and seemed unhappy, especially with me; our close relationship was shifting into something both upsetting and unrecognizable. Nick was moody and at times downright rude. I was being pushed away, much like that first day of kindergarten, but now it seemed personal and abruptly painful.

I was very aware that there was a shift from parenting my

child to now parenting my adult child. Mothering doesn't end at this stage. It takes a different approach and requires one to really step back. It becomes a relationship of partnering and support, from a distance. No baby book had prepared me for this transition, and there were times when I felt completely lost as to how to navigate through it. Growing up, Nick was required to fit into our family's life, and I took that for granted. When he became an adult, I had to sit back, observe, and learn how I would now fit into his life. Where once we had a close bond, with lots of communication, there was now a gap of empty spaces. I missed him and our times together and I felt hurt by his behaviour. But I understood that this was necessary and continued to hope we'd eventually find a way that felt comfortable for both of us.

I wanted to do what was right; I wanted to be the kind of mom who could just let go, and I worked hard to do so. But what I soon learned was that defining this and understanding what it should look like can be a timely and somewhat messy struggle.

Chapter 8

Nick and Jake return to school for second semester. Some time passes and then Jake calls and invites Brian and I to Guelph for dinner. He has forgotten some things at home and we agree to bring them with us. Our role now seems very superficial; the brief closeness I felt during our trip home from Mexico has quickly waned, and Jake has been distant, with little communication until now.

When asked about school Jake claims to be very focused on his studies and says the workload has increased. He is not jubilant or excited; he just seems to be going through the motions. We exchange paperwork and computer supplies and then drive away, not suspecting that Jake could be having problems dealing with school.

Jake comes to our family home for back-to-back Family Day weekend and Reading Week in February. He seems happier and relieved to have a break. We spend little time together, though, and Jake shares that he's glad that Brian and I have been able to spend more time with each other, as empty nesters. I have created a life for myself outside of motherhood, and am also very active with work, friends, and my community. Over the course of the week I do notice that Jake is spending a lot of time in his bedroom and on his computer, late at night, playing video games, seemingly non-stop. I'm a little annoyed by it but let the fact that I'm happy to have him home override my frustration. I say nothing. After all, he's an adult now, and just a visitor in our home. I seem to have little say in his life now. Although I do understand the need for us to create some separation and space from each other, I am feeling sad and disconnected, and somewhat confused as to what my role as a mother now is. There is less hands-on nurturing and guidance, but he is still my son, and there is still a need to partner and be supportive. I am still struggling with both Nick and Jake to define what this now means, and I have to admit to myself that I feel a bit lost.

In March, after spending another weekend with Jake at home, I approach him about his exam schedule, and realize suddenly that he will be done his first year of university by April 10th. The time has flown by quickly. I feel satisfied that Jake's first year appears to be a success, despite the changes I have noticed in his behaviour over the course of the two semesters. It is not just his tenacious and petulant attitude towards me that has been bothersome. There were times in second semester I would drive to Guelph to pick him up and he would still be sleeping in the early or late afternoon, not being ready for pick-up. He started to appear at his door with a terrible body odour, even his clothing smelled, and his hair was greasy. I thought it was odd that he would let his grooming slip, but I also remembered that as a small boy he always hated bathing, and he had a lax attitude about how he looked. I thought maybe he was regressing a bit. After all, he was really busy with his studies and staying up late to finish assignments on time; perhaps he had just reverted to his boyish habits. Thinking it is the right thing to do, I choose to step back and allow him to grow at his pace and under his terms. The nurturer in me wants to coddle and check in with Jake more often, reminding him to manage his time better. But my need to prove that I can let go supersedes this urge. I wonder to myself if, in my need to please Jake, I may perhaps be ignoring the warning signs of a storm to come.

Chapter 9

I was enjoying an outdoor winter party with my husband, Brian, and our son, Nicholas, chatting with friends, and someone asked, "Will you and Brian be having another child?"

I remember my answer so distinctly. I replied, "No, we're not planning to have another child for at least another year. Nicholas is three years old now and more independent; we're just enjoying some romance again in our marriage."

It was true, we'd had this discussion earlier that week and we were both happy with waiting. Motherhood had been especially difficult for me for the first two years and I was happy now to be feeling much more confident and stable. Brian and I had more time to spend together, and we wanted to capitalize on that opportunity. But we were definitely looking forward to having another child eventually and a sibling for Nicholas.

About two weeks later I remember standing at the kitchen sink, washing dishes, when I was suddenly overcome with a familiar nauseous feeling in the pit of my belly. Later that week, the doctor confirmed that I was pregnant again. Waiting another twelve months was no longer an option, and

I immersed myself immediately in the joy of growing a second child in my belly. I couldn't be happier.

This pregnancy was much easier than the first; it was the delivery that was more of a challenge. This baby was in a bit of a rush to arrive, coming two weeks before the due date. After a few hours of labour and just a couple of quick pushes from me, our baby boy flew out, way too fast, and clipped his shoulder against my tailbone. The pain was searing! Tears of agony were mixed with tears of happiness; we had another healthy son. We named him Jacob. He was just one ounce bigger than his big brother and just as beautiful.

We all instantly fell in love with Jacob. Nicholas was over the moon about having a baby brother, and he was so good with him from the very beginning. I spent my first six weeks, post-partum, sitting on a coccyx cushion to heal my tailbone. I know it's cliché to say that your child can be a pain in the butt, but at that time, mine most definitely was. In no time, my lower back felt better, and the first few months of caring for Jake came more easily. I had more confidence, this time, as a mother.

At five months old, Jacob came down with what appeared to be stomach influenza and lost three pounds. The doctor didn't seem too concerned at that time, but over the next several months it appeared that Jacob was not rebounding back to full health. He developed a deep cough that would cause his little body to shake. He then began to suffer with chronic diarrhea, and at times projectile vomiting and his skin would break out in rashes and hives. He was pale and anemic, and his growth slowed down considerably. He eventually plummeted from the ninety percentile on his baby growth chart to below the twenty-five percentile, and then his growth plateaued for six months. Strangely and ironically, the family doctor believed he would grow out of this phase, choosing to offer no medical solution. We took matters into our own hands and got a referral to a gastro specialist in the top children's hospital in the city through a doctor friend of ours. Jacob was beginning to lose muscle mass in his thighs by the time he was finally seen. Many tests were done, including a bowel biopsy, but the results were inconclusive, leaving the doctors baffled, and my husband and I fraught with fear and inadequacy. The medical system was not working in our favour. Jacob was withdrawn, quiet, lethargic and continued to remain underweight.

Months later, with still no answers, during a two-week period three different people suggested to me to seek the help of a holistic health practitioner who specialized in something called Iridology. I had never heard of this, but after the third person urged me, I took it as a sign. I was desperate to get help for my child and really had nothing to lose by looking at a complimentary modality. I did some research and learned that Iridology is the science of reading the nerves within the iris to assess the nutritional health in the body, and I was open and willing to meet with this person to have Jake assessed.

Although it is not a tool used for diagnosis, seeing the core of nutritional deficiencies can be helpful. The Iridologist believed Jake's large intestines to be inflamed, and that both Yeast and Staphylococcus bacteria had settled there. Jacob's diet was restricted to alkaline foods, and we added an age-old herbal remedy called Slippery Elm powder to his food to literally soothe and put out the fire in his belly. Live bacterial culture in the form of Probiotics powder was also included to restore the bacterial flora in his gut.

Within a couple of weeks we saw enormous improvements in Jacob's health; the diarrhea stopped, the cough lessened in intensity, his skin cleared, and he began to gain weight. The gastro specialist called me at home to discuss tests results done before we began this new course of action. Once again, the test didn't reveal anything. As she was discussing our next move, I explained to her that we had seen an

Iridologist and shared her assessment and recommendations.

The doctor immediately said, "That's impossible; Staph infection doesn't ever reach the bowels."

I then expressed how well Jacob was responding and how much better he was doing.

She then said, "I take that back. Doctors have never been able to prove that Staph infection doesn't reach the bowels. Whatever you are doing now for your son, I approve. The medical field has obviously not been helpful. Keep doing what you're doing, and if you require me in the future do not hesitate to make an appointment."

I was grateful for this admission and honesty from a medical doctor and thanked her for all she'd done to help. I hung up the phone finally feeling hopeful that our son was going to be well again.

There was no looking back; Jacob thrived again, both physically and emotionally. That placid little toddler gained weight and caught back up on the growth chart over the next six months. And as his body grew and strengthened, so did his personality, in big ways! He suddenly became a child of great determination, with a lot of time to make up for. He became tenacious and defiant, typical of a two-year-old, but with more ferocity. He hungered for food and for physical activity, and I could barely keep up with him. It was as though I had to get to know who Jacob was all over again; a new person was evolving before me, and this person required a different approach than the one used with a fragile sickly child. It was wonderful, and it was a relief, and it was a very busy time for both of us.

This event woke me up to the fact that our medical system is fallible, and that Jake had nearly slipped through the cracks of a less than stellar system. Thankfully I was able to catch him before he fell through and became more ill, or worse. My advocating for Jake became highlighted, and it was vital that I sought a different method to regain his health. It would not be the last time Jake's unique needs would have him slip through a loosely structured system. The road ahead was filled with barriers that would require close observation, determination and inventiveness.

Chapter 10

Mid-April my husband and I return to Guelph, load Jake's belongings into our vehicle, and bring him to our home for the summer. He offers to take us out to his favourite restaurant and pay for a celebratory dinner that night; we are so touched. This gesture seems so grown up and we accept. Over dinner, Jake tells us that his first year at Guelph U has been a success and that he has passed all of his courses. He has decided that he will work at the pub as their dishwasher for the summer and that he has already requested more hours from his boss. He is only given one weeknight and weekend shifts at first, and I assume this will pick up when the outdoor patio opens in warmer weather.

In the meantime, Jake prepares for a very important trip he is taking to meet up with a friend whom he met online back when he was twelve years old. They have nurtured their friendship over the Internet for six years now, and are going to meet for the first time, in person, in Japan. Brian and I are not naïve about this, and have done our homework, having already established contact with this friend and his family, and feel confident that this will be a safe adventure. We are excited about Jake travelling alone for the first time and believe that it will be an excellent experience for him.

Jake continues to stay up late playing video games and starts sleeping through the day, awaking late afternoon most days. I let it slide for a bit, thinking he needs a break from routine after a year away at university. By May I start noticing that Jake's body is very twitchy, and he seems quite agitated. He says that his neck is really bothering him, so I arrange for him to have treatments with a chiropractor. After a few appointments he tells me he feels it is helping, but he's still shaky and edgy. I assume it is the nervousness about his first trip on his own, to a place quite far away. Again, I let it slide. Mid-May Jake leaves for Tokyo, Japan. A day after he leaves we hear that he has arrived safely, and as his trip unfolds he keeps us posted with emails and photographs of various landmarks they are visiting. He sounds happy and we are delighted for him. I am especially pleased and surprised that Jake is communicating so much while away, a far cry from the cooler shoulder I received while he was attending school. I'm not going to lie, I had all of the normal worries any parent would have, from Jake losing his passport to the guys being pickpocketed or worse, getting hurt. I stayed in touch with Jake's friend's mother via email the entire time, and we helped each other to stay positive about the journey.

Eleven days later Jake returns from his trip, ecstatic and super confident for having taken this very big holiday, without us. We are so proud for him for handling himself so well on this first solo journey. He tells us all about it. We're relieved that he's home, and that the holiday was such a great experience.

~~~~~~

In June, despite my urgings, Jake is still not actively looking for more summer work, and is only working part time at the pub. He's opened up and is communicating much more, suddenly delightful company, helping me with some gardening and coming along to help with errands, and I am enjoying our conversations. The mood between us seems to have lightened since he's returned home from Japan. He is still spending much more time than I am happy with, playing a lot of video games and talking with friends online into the early morning hours.

I eventually broach the subject and he becomes furious with me, and justifies his behaviour by yelling at me, "This will be my last free time before university co-op kicks in. Then I will either work or be in school every summer, and I just want to be able to enjoy myself."

His outburst catches me by surprise, but I do understand what he is trying to convey. I know that once he finishes school and begins to work full time that there will be no more of these four-month breaks and playtime will be reduced considerably. I share this conversation with Brian and he agrees that there's no need to push Jake, and to let him have his last easy summer. I don't want to sever the calm Jake and I have been experiencing in our relationship lately, and so I relent. But something inside me is questioning my better judgement. I'm uncomfortable with the relentless hours he's spending online. I keep telling myself that he's an adult, after all, and isn't this when I should back off and allow my adult child to spread his wings and fly? Brian's mother was overprotective and constantly telling him what to do and continues to try to do so now. He wants me to back off and leave Jake to make his own decisions, just as he wishes his own mother would do. My parents were the exact opposite and became aloof in their approach to parenting once I turned eighteen, so I am torn. I am constantly questioning just how much I should push and encourage and how much I should just let go of. My husband and I are contributing to some of the cost of Jake's university education, and he is living under our roof, so we have rights. Do we treat him as a rent-free boarder and have no expectations? He has been helping around the house and he has been speaking more kindly. He's not doing drugs, or drinking a lot of alcohol, and he's not involved in criminal activity; he's an intelligent and decent young man. I quiet the discontent inside of me, and somehow convince myself to loosen the reigns.

Throughout the rest of the summer Jake makes an effort to be more social when he's not connected online to his computer. He visits with his brother in the city, he plays a little tennis with his dad and they see a professional baseball game together. He opts out of volunteering at the tennis masters tournament this year, complaining that the heat is too much for him. His brother also chooses to miss it, so it's not a big deal. Jake helps set up for a milestone celebration for his grandmother's 100th birthday and is his usual charming and delightful self at the party. Jake spends some time on errands with me and we always have fantastic conversations, always mixed with our serious thoughts and with humour. I love how deeply Jake thinks and feels, and I enjoy his company immensely. He can make me be more reflective and he can make me laugh out loud. He is never late for his work shifts and works with great enthusiasm on the job. He is loved by the staff.

In July I take Jake to the orthodontist for a consultation for braces, and then in August he has them installed. This is a very exciting moment for Jake, as he has been unhappy with his teeth and the shape of his mouth for a long time. In August Brian and I make an impulsive decision to adopt a pair of small dogs from the local pound. We bring them home and Jake is so happy. He has missed his little Yorkie who passed over a year ago. The dogs give him a new purpose, and he starts helping me with training, which ultimately gets Jake on a better daytime routine, with fewer late nights on his computer. At the end of August Jake and his brother prepare for me a delicious, early birthday dinner, before Jake is to head back into university residence. It's a fabulous night, Myles has joined us, the dinner is exceptional, and I am filled with love and attention from both of my sons. It feels like things are momentarily settled and it's good between us at last. It is my deepest desire that this moment of peace and satisfaction will last, but I am not certain it can.

Chapter 11

As Jacob got a little older we shortened his name to Jake because he preferred it. Anytime one of us slipped into calling him Jacob, he swiftly reminded us that it was Jake. The name Jacob quickly became a thing of the past. Just before Jake's fourth birthday, I considered sending him to an independent day care program so that he could earn some independence and socialize more with other children, as the junior kindergarten program in the school system had been withdrawn that year. I found a program that ran half-days and enrolled Jake in the fall. To say the least, it was a disaster.

Within the program there was time to play. That wasn't a problem. But there were also expectations for doing schoolwork; primary exercises with printing the alphabet and numbers. Each day I would wait outside in the hall with the other mothers while the children were dismissed, and every few days Jake's irritated teacher would hold up his paper with a big red X on it and exclaim that Jake refused to do his work that day. I had two opinions about this. First, I felt it was detrimental for the woman to be expressing her feelings about this, not only in front of Jake, but also in front of the other mothers and children. It was a form of humiliation, and I didn't approve. Secondly, I didn't see why it was such a big deal. Jake wasn't even four years old yet. He had plenty of time for this kind of learning. I had enrolled him to engage in some social activity. I tolerated it for a few weeks, and then took the caregiver aside and asked her if Jake was being disruptive when the other children were doing their written exercises.

"No, Jake just sits quietly in his chair during that time," she replied.

I knew how stubborn Jake could now be and could just imagine him refusing to do the work in a sort of passive aggressive manner, and found it amusing that he could wield so much power over this woman. It was apparent that it bothered her, and she obviously wanted more control. But, quite frankly, it wasn't a big deal to me. The purpose of Jake's attendance was to integrate him into a social setting with peers of his age and to have time to play. I was not going to waste time forcing him to do something he wasn't either ready for or was simply uninterested in, or both, especially since he wasn't disturbing anyone.

Before the Christmas break Jake started expressing his dislike of the program, and then he became quite ill and developed pneumonia, and I sensed that the daycare program wasn't the best place for Jake to be. If I thought that the teachers were condescending with me, they were probably even worse with Jake. He was clearly unhappy and not ready. Although Nick had been the kind of child who couldn't get out the door fast enough to be in a school setting, it was becoming clear that Jake just wasn't like him in this regard. And I was really okay with that.

We waited until the next fall, and Jake began senior kindergarten. Completely opposite to his brother, he was more than accepting and happy to have his mother drive him to school on the first day. In fact, he requested that I remain in the classroom with him for his first afternoon of elementary school. The teacher was very understanding and allowed a few of us to stay. Jake didn't fall into the school routine easily at first and insisted that I volunteer in the classroom as a helper. I was happy to do this if it would make integration easier for him. Jake had a wonderful teacher who made the process of learning fun for him, and Jake was willing to co-operate. He made friends easily and learned to print letters and numbers, and eventually his own name. At the end of the year, he seemed to be doing just fine.

~~~~~~~~~~~~~~~~~~~~~~~~~~~~~~~~~~~~~

Grade one came the following September, and the seesaw of school learning that would become Jake's nemesis reared its ugly head again. The controlling teacher issue was again upon us, only I didn't see it right away. Jake wasn't providing me with any details, but within the second week of school he started complaining about stomach pains and bad dreams, and he wanted to stay at home rather than attend school. Again, I agreed to be a volunteer in his classroom to help ease his comfort level. I thought that this was behind us after a successful year in kindergarten. But now, it was no longer half days; Jake was attending full days that perhaps would take him more time to adapt to.

By week four, I witnessed something rather disturbing in the class while volunteering my time. Each morning the teacher had the children sit in a circle on the floor for "Circle Time", and the teacher read and then asked them questions about the story. They were expected to sit up, with backs straight and their hands folded in their laps the entire time. The teacher would watch and remind them of posture each time a child moved out of his/her expected position. This performance by the teacher and the children lasted for forty-five minutes. Now, I am no early childhood expert, nor am I a teacher, but raising two children of my own, I knew that having a child of six sit perfectly still for even five minutes was a challenge. Even adults don't want to do this for forty-five minutes. And boys are active; they learn through physical movement far more than girls do. Jake was no exception. In fact, Jake rarely sat still; he was very tactile, and his body was twitchy and seemingly in constant, subtle motion. At home, we didn't take issue with this; he was free to move as he needed. He behaved well; he wasn't climbing walls or destroying property, he was just being a little boy, exploring his world in his own way.

During circle time Jake wasn't sitting perfectly still. He was twisting his hands and rocking gently, and suddenly I heard the teacher snap, "Jake, if you don't stop moving, I will remove your shirt."

"She will remove a piece of his clothing, and have him sit shirtless in the circle," I thought. Did she believe that she could humiliate him into sitting still? That's ridiculous, and inappropriate, and a little emotionally abusive to me. I was furious with her threat. I didn't want to embarrass Jake, so I waited until the class broke for outdoor recess before approaching his teacher about this.

I asked her, "If Jake had continued doing what you didn't like, would you have followed through with your threat?"

"Absolutely," she replied.

"Well, I'm not comfortable with that," I returned.

Putting her hand to her throat, as though she were somehow protecting it, she then asked, "Why not?"

"Well, think about it," I replied, "If I made the same threat to you, how would you feel?"

And my brain just spun with disbelief as she retorted with, "That's different. I'm a woman."

I quickly responded, "No, you're a person, and so is Jake, and he deserves the same kind of respect that you require."

She had no response; I left her speechless, and returned to my duties, waiting for the children to re-enter the class. I had made my point. There was nothing else left to say. But inside I was still reeling with anger.

That same day after school, she approached me, and started to tell me that she'd had a bad day and that her car had been hit in the parking lot, and then she began to cry. She made no apology for her earlier outburst with Jake but was looking for some kind of sympathy from me about her own dilemma. I wasn't sure if she was using this as an attempt to excuse her behaviour that morning or if she was just a fragile person who had lost control of her emotions in the moment. Either way, the situation left me uncomfortable, and I felt that if she were that unstable then perhaps she needed some support from administration.

I made a phone call to the principal and didn't lodge a formal complaint, but rather explained what had happened with my son in the classroom, and then the emotional outburst the teacher had later shared. I then suggested that maybe she needed some sort of conversation and support from him. He thanked me for the call and said that he would speak with her.

It didn't seem to get a whole lot better after that, not only for Jake but for the rest of the students, as well. It was just days later that I received a telephone call from one of the other volunteer mothers in that classroom. She was calling to tell me that the teacher seemed to be picking on my child and went on to say that she'd witnessed the teacher's outburst that morning when Jake had been fidgeting with his sock while sitting at his desk. She said that the teacher snatched the sock off his foot and then she smashed it on his desk. She then placed her face an inch away from Jake's and began to scream at him. I was so incensed upon hearing this, and immediately realized that my discussion with the principal had not helped whatsoever. My child was still being bullied in her classroom and needed my help again. I appreciated having an inside, objective view and would be watching things closely the following day when my next volunteer shift began.

The following morning this teacher was in a particularly foul mood, and before I had any opportunity to speak with her about Jake, she went into a rage with another child, and as I watched in horror I could see that her anger seemed to take on a life of its own. She was far too quick to show her temper, and once she did, her face became inflamed with heat, and all common sense disappeared. There was no stopping the verbal diarrhea that she spewed, and it was very alarming to see how little she was in control. I could now see, very clearly, how frightened Jake must be feeling while in school. I made my decision in that moment to have Jake permanently removed from her classroom.

My husband and I were united in our decision and together we met with the principal in his office, the following day. There was not another school Jake could attend in our district. I would ultimately be responsible for Jake's Grade One education. I decided that I would homeschool him for the remainder of the school year.

I began to understand that in both the daycare and the Grade One experiences, the teachers seemed to have only one method for teaching. There was no room for accommodating the individual needs of the student. Here was another situation in which advocacy and intervention were necessary for Jake's best interest. Jake moved and twitched and appeared to be very tactile in his approach to learning. Sitting still at a desk, listening and working with pencil and paper were uncomfortable for him. While I homeschooled, he was not required to be still, but was instead encouraged to move and explore, and we spent a great deal of his learning outside of our home and on field trips, where he could have hands-on experiences. We still managed to get printing, spelling, reading, math, and phonics exercises done, but it was during play that Jake seemed to absorb the most information. Homeschooling was a learning experience for me, as I had no formal teaching credentials, but we muddled along and figured it out as best we could. Jake continued to tell me that he didn't ever want to go back to school. I wasn't sure that I wanted to continue homeschooling, and Jake would eventually need a setting with peers of his age. Brian and I were both wary of what sort of teacher he'd receive the following year, but it was definitely worth an attempt at re-integrating him into school in the fall.

Chapter 12

At the end of August 2014, we move Jake back to the University of Guelph to his new residence. This time he is way off campus, in a townhouse residence with two other male students. He has his own room and a shared kitchen, common area, and bathroom. He asks us to take him grocery shopping, deciding that he's going to take more interest in cooking and stock up his cupboard and fridge with lots of food. I am impressed that he wants to cook, since he has also taken a meal plan for this school year. But I am also surprised, as Jake loved the meal plan last year, and the second-year program is going to require much more of his time and focus. I don't know how he'll be organized enough to prepare meals. Regardless, we help him to get food and supplies and take them back to his new home. He seems very happy to be back at school, and as we finish unpacking and get ready to leave, Jake plunks down on his favourite beanbag chair and gives us a look of utter satisfaction. We leave for home feeling good. Saying good-bye to Jake this school year feels easier than it did the year before.

I get busy with fall gardening and clients I'm seeing, and I don't hear much from Jake. I assume he's busy sorting out his new school schedule. Brian and I help move Nick and Myles into their new rental in the Junction. Renting an apartment is a really big step for Nick; his first place and also a move in with his girlfriend. I welcome having something to celebrate with

Nick to break up some of the tension that has been brewing between us for too long. He's graduated now from university and is doing a paid internship with a social media company. He loves the job and is confident that it will become a full-time permanent position at the end of the term. Nick couldn't be happier moving into his own apartment. He has dreamed of this moment for a long time, and he's ready for the responsibility. I have no worries about how he'll handle a budget, pay his bills, make meals, and keep his home safe and clean. This will be so much fun for both he and Myles. We elicit help from friends and collect used furniture to fill some of their space. And we provide them with the contents of the kitchen Brian had when he rented his own small apartment while working in New York a few years back. He had stored these items in the basement for just this occasion. Nick decides to give up his car now; he is ready to fully embrace the city life and looks forward to commuting using the transit system. I didn't think I'd ever see him give up this freedom. But I realize that being in the city without a car provides him with the sense that he is completely separate and far removed from his childhood home in the country, and that in itself is freeing.

A couple weeks later Jake takes transit to Toronto to see Nick's new apartment, and meets up with Brian, Nick, Myles, and I for dinner. We then attend the Black Keys concert together; a Christmas present I had purchased earlier and that we were all really looking forward to. We have an absolute blast, the performance is excellent, and it's a happy family get-together.

Jake continues to spend more time in the city with Nick and Myles, and I start wondering how he is managing to have the time to travel to the city and get his school assignments done. When I inquire, he tells me that year two is not nearly as difficult as he thought it might be. Jake is very bright, and he has been doing computer coding recreationally for quite some time, so I assume that he is smart enough to handle the course load.

Early October, and Jake meets us again in Toronto, this time to celebrate his dad's birthday. The transit ride for Jake is over two hours long. Seems excessive to me, but he says that it gives him time to read and study. We meet for dinner, and although it's a special occasion and we're eating at a more formal restaurant, I notice that Jake's grooming has slid again, he looks thin, and he smells funky. He's not taking care of his teeth as well as he should, either, especially since his orthodontist work. This time I have to say something, as we are picking up the tab for both the dinner and his orthodontic work. He promises to take better care in future, but says that school is very busy, and he is rushing to classes all the time.

The following week I drive to Guelph and bring Jake back to our home for his 19th birthday. Once again, he looks and smells bad. He's lost more weight, his pupils are dilated, he looks tired, and his complexion has broken out. I take him into my clinic to do a health check. I have a practice in Holistic Health and specialize in Iridology. I note that since he's gotten braces and started second year at school, he's lost 11.5 lbs. He says it's more difficult to eat now with braces. I do an assessment and see that his thyroid seems out of balance and I give him a remedy for this. I also take him to the health store to get some protein powder to have for breakfast to add weight back on. He's pale and shaky but says there are no problems with school; in fact, he continues to maintain that it's really easy. The following night Jake complains of fatigue and headache, asks to be excused and then goes to bed early. Now I am concerned. He is not looking healthy and I worry that the course load at school is perhaps too much, despite what Jake is telling me. Brian and I discuss this and he reminds me how much pressure there is in university, and that maybe Jake is just feeling some of the burden. He is not as worried as I am.

Before he heads back to university, Jake asks me for some of my homemade soups to take with him. I find this very strange because Jake refused them last school year and told me the meal plan at Guelph was amazing. I mention this, and Jake explains that my soup is easier to eat with braces. It still seems strange to me; don't they sell soup in the cafeteria, I wonder.

I am so flattered that he wants something I have made lovingly at home, and so I pack some up for him. I start thinking a lot about Jake and notice that he doesn't seem to have homework when he visits on weekends. He's continuing to lose weight, he looks unwell and stressed. He also doesn't answer my texts until many hours after I send them, if he answers them at all. Sometimes I have to re-send them to get answers. Something doesn't feel quite right, but I can't put a finger on it. I ask questions, and Jake seems to have an answer and justification for every one of them.

~~~~~~~~~~~~~~~~~~~~~~~~~~~~~~~~~~~~~~~

Later in the month, I drive to Guelph with soups, stews, and lasagna I have prepared for Jake. He is thrilled with this delivery, and says he misses me, that he's eating better, and gaining weight and sleeping better. I hadn't realized that sleep was an issue until now, but he somehow does look a little better.

As I am standing in the common area, I notice a terrible odour in the residence and I ask, "What is that awful smell?"

"Oh, it's because I haven't taken out my garbage and recycling in a couple of weeks," he says.

"Oh, Jake, that is a horrible odour. Let's pack up your garbage and recycling and I'll drive you around to the bins and you can drop it off before we go to dinner."

He hesitates, and so I move to the door and walk into his room. I am shocked at the mess, and the smell is ghastly. I see a small stack of pizza boxes in the corner, and that makes no sense to me. Pizza is sold on campus so why is he having it delivered to his room?

"Why are you ordering in pizza and not getting your dinner with your meal plan?" I inquire.

"I'm so busy with school work at night that I have no time to go to campus for food. It's a long walk from here."

I listen to his explanation and he sounds convincing, but something in me doesn't feel right about it. For fear of upsetting Jake and coming across as nosy and untrusting, I don't ask more questions. Instead, I help him pack up and get the rancid garbage out of his room.

We head to dinner and Jake is over-the-top exuberant, very talkative, very sweet, and I relax and enjoy his company, easily forgetting about my concerns and questions.

Through the next week I text Jake and notice he answers me at 3:00 in the morning again. My sixth sense is kicking in and I believe something is really not right. I ask him if he is even attending classes, suggesting that he has appeared to be quite a night owl for the past several weeks. He assures me he is going to classes but has had some assignments keeping him up at night. Everything about it doesn't feel right, and I'm not sure I can trust his answers anymore. I decide I am going to start paying closer attention and look for more evidence of a possible issue.

Chapter 13

After Jake's year of being homeschooled, I was discussing my concerns with a friend about whether Jake was going to be Grade Two ready. I was also concerned because Jake continued saying that he didn't want to go back to school. Had I taught him enough and had he learned enough to be ready for the next grade? At this time, my friend suggested that I take Jake to be tested by a professional outside of the school.

I did my research and found a psychologist who did intellectual and educational testing. I booked an appointment for Jake for the following week. This kindly gentleman spent a couple of hours with my son, putting him through various exercises before he emerged from the office and invited Brian and I in to discuss his findings.

He said that many times throughout the testing Jake had asked him if what he was asking was a trick question, and he found that quite amusing coming from a seven-year-old boy. He also informed us that he found that Jake was of gifted intelligence, with a high IQ, and that he would eventually need to be placed in a gifted program in school to challenge him. He would otherwise become bored in school if he remained in a core program. This news came as quite a relief to my husband and I. Although we felt that Jake was a smart little boy, the issues we'd experienced in school thus far had made us question a lot of things. Jake had really struggled in grade one, but we weren't sure if it was as a result of the duress he felt with the teacher, or if there was some sort of learning disability. This was good news. We left the meeting feeling satisfied, and ready to enroll Jake back into school. We then explained to him, in simple terms that he would understand that the psychologist had found him to be very smart.

A couple weeks later, while in the car, from the back seat I heard Jake say to me, "Mommy, I want to go back to school now."

This surprised me, and so I asked him, "What changed your mind about school?"

And Jake replied, "Because now I know that I am smart."

I was left with two distinct feelings. One was relief, as I felt that returning to school would be beneficial for Jake. The second feeling was one of sadness. All of those months of homeschooling I had told Jake on so many occasions what a smart child he was, and yet he never believed me. He had somehow equated his awful experience in Grade One and possibly nursery school with not being smart. It took the psychologist and the results of his test for Jake to finally believe he was clever. His school experience had left him without confidence, and no amount of praise from me had changed that. I suddenly felt enormous sadness for the many children before Jake who had a teacher inadvertently leave them feeling dumb, and that without this sort of testing or intervention, they might go through their entire school career, and perhaps even their lives, believing that they were not smart. All of that potential lost; these intelligent children falling through the cracks in the school system due to one early negative experience. I felt heartbroken. And at the same time, I felt grateful again that Jake was caught before he fell further.

This didn't mean that Jake would return to school and have it easy. With his high IQ he was an intellectual minority and didn't fit into the mould that the school system constructed for him. Jake was not a typical visual or audio learner either; his learning style was found, through further testing, to be tactile/kinesthetic, and therefore sitting for long periods of time at a desk was not an ideal method for having him take in and retain information. He needed to be able to move to learn and be in a setting where hands-on sensory experience would be offered. Jake's school success would be built on ongoing parent-teacher meetings, parental advocacy, and modifications to his learning. As his mother and in charge of much of his care, I had my work cut out for me.

Grade school required a great deal of focus for both Jake and I. His challenge was due to the difficult task of learning in an environment not always conducive to his needs, while mine was in observing where and when my input was needed to help. I recognized that it was not easy to teach a class of twenty-five or more children who have different needs and learning styles, and so I was careful not to hover and become overly-protective. I assessed each situation that arose and did what I could to support both the teachers and Jake. I had, after all, spent Grade One teaching Jake from home, and knew it took a very different approach; he was not the easiest student. He wasn't disruptive, nor did he behave badly in school, but despite his intelligence, learning could be somewhat burdensome for him. It didn't always come easy like it had for his older brother. Reading was one of Jake's biggest challenges. If given a large chunk of reading at once, he would become so overwhelmed that he'd freeze and stop trying to read at all. He began to hate reading. I wanted him to have a love of books, so I decided, at home, to give Jake a different type of genre to read, one that was broken down into smaller bits and included more pictures. I started with comic books. I loved Gary Larson's Far Side humour and had on occasion shared his cartoons with Jake and Nick. They both understood and loved his farcical cartoons. So, I provided Jake with one of his books, and rather than reading pages at a time, he could read one funny frame at a time. This worked, and then we moved onto the Calvin and Hobbes cartoon series, at the suggestion of a friend. Eventually Jake learned to like reading, and developed quite a sense of humour, as well. It was never easy, and I needed to be both patient and imaginative. Beyond the classroom work, there was Jake's immense struggle with doing homework assignments. Often, he found them tedious, unnecessary, boring and time-consuming. He had better things to do. In all honesty there were assignments that were nonsensical to me, and I had no rational explanation as to what purpose they served. I understood that sometimes one just had to grind through to completion even what one didn't enjoy. Learning wasn't always going to be fun for Jake, and I eventually found myself repeating the same mantra to him: "Just play the game and do the work."

Chapter 14

On Halloween Day, I am sitting in my living room at home watching some afternoon TV, and my phone buzzes with an incoming email. It is from Jake. I don't know it yet, but my world is about to be rocked. As I read through his lengthy email, disbelief starts to set in. Jake explains a scary situation that he's gotten into. He's created a lie so deep that he is now backed into a corner and in need of my help. Every bone in my body is telling me not to panic; this situation is delicate, and Jake is feeling vulnerable and desperate. He needs me to be calm and understanding. As I continue to read the message I am overwhelmed and very aware that this situation could have gone another way, and the message could have been delivered to me too late, and by a stranger.

The email reads as follows:

I've got to say something: I've panicked and fallen on my face. This semester due to my own mistakes I've ended up pretty much losing the semester.

I messed up on course selection last year for this semester, and then when it finally came time for me to pick courses, there was only 1 available. I registered for it and thought "okay, I can talk to the course counsellor about the others next, let's see how this goes" but mixed up the tuition payment deadline and ended up paying my tuition late. This led to me getting unregistered from the only course

I had, and that was the final nail in the coffin. I panicked, and my anxiety took over from there, driving me further and further into recluse. Every time I thought about reaching out for help, my mind just drove me back into constant questions of "what if there is no help? What if it's too late?" And that fear of learning if there wasn't help was enough to cause me to not want to get an answer at all. I freaked out and just couldn't bring myself past this mental barrier.

I tried really hard to do it on my own, to solve these problems myself, but I couldn't. I didn't realize just how bad my anxiety could get, and how much it could really affect me. I tried to be strong for you and dad, I didn't want you to worry about me and think you had to dote on me because of it, and that's been the reason I've tried so hard over the years to improve my anxiety and get control of it. I couldn't do it on my own, and it's cost me. I've lost this semester because of it.

At the start of October, I did finally manage to own up to my fears and set up an appointment with the program counsellor about my situation. We made a plan and I wouldn't have completely wasted my first semester of second year. The plan was made on the Friday, so I was going to go to the offices to begin fixing things the Monday after dad's birthday weekend. I set my alarm to wake myself up on time for it, but my phone died because I had no charger and the battery life ran out. I woke up when the offices were already closed, and it threw me back into my panic. Instead of just going on the Tuesday and fixing things, my fears worsened, and I found myself unable to move from my room. Finally, my Residence Assistant (RA) came to the building to ask me about everything because all the information they had was that I wasn't registered, and I was forced to talk about the situation. There wasn't any pressure on my head talking to her, so I took the chance to talk about everything that had happened.

I went with her to a drop-in session with a therapist in the University Center so that I could get help, and the counsellor finally started making me understand just what it was that made me tick, and where my anxiety came from. It was really helpful, and I know now that this issue I have isn't something that I can face alone or have to face alone. I wanted to show I was strong but my interpretation of what strong really is false in the worst of ways. I then immediately afterwards talked to my program counsellor about course selection and my professor for that one course I started out in. It's too late to jump into the course, and it can't be compressed down into a single month's time because it's so oriented around group work. I'm talking with the program counsellor again on Monday next week at 2pm to register for next semester and figure out a plan for how I can get all the courses back and fix this mess.

I'm sorry I lied to you and dad and everyone else about being fine. I really wasn't fine; I was the farthest thing from it. I was so scared that you would all be disappointed, angry, or just ashamed of my mistakes. I didn't want you guys to have to deal with it all, so I stupidly took it all upon myself to try and fix but I couldn't. I'm so sorry for messing up like this, for tossing all your trust out the window again and for stomping on the lessons you worked so hard to teach me about always having help available. I never meant to cause so much trouble again, I didn't want to avoid everything, but I just felt so cornered. I wanted to be in university so badly and I still want to take courses this semester, but I couldn't beat my own mental barricade of fears to solve the issues preventing me from fixing everything. I'm sorry.

I'm going to be taking courses again next semester. I won't let this lost semester slow me down or stop me, but it's going to be a hindrance that will cause me to have to really work to make up for it. The problem now is that I have to move out of residence for the rest of the semester because technically I won't be registered again until the start of next semester. I have to move out Monday or Tuesday next week and move back in at the start of semester 2. I can't hide any of this anymore, and I never should have hid it all in the first place. If I had just told you about the issue from the very beginning, told anyone, I would have been able to get the support and help I needed. I messed up so badly and it's been really scary trying to hold myself together alone these past two months and not breaking down in front of you, dad, or Nick when I really needed to. I don't want smiling to hurt anymore. I can only hope you can forgive me for all this.

I'm sorry

I am stunned as I read through the email.

My mind is left paralyzed with one thought.

I know instinctively that there was a good chance Jake could have chosen to not come clean and confess, and instead check out of this world completely. Just two weeks prior to this I was reading an article on a young med student who wasn't making the grades and felt that he was such a failure and couldn't face disappointing his parents with the truth, so he took his own life. That story is screaming in my head right now, and I see how close Jake's situation could have come to this. But he didn't run away from the issue today, he chose courage, he chose to face it head on, and I am so grateful, literally, that he is alive! That is all that I can think about, so much that I can barely comprehend the entire situation he is describing in the email. I am overtaken with a sense that Jake's mental state is on the edge and hanging on my reaction to this message. He needs me, and I need to be there for him, regardless of what has transpired. I know this with every fiber of my being.

Jake is in real trouble and in a very vulnerable state, and without really understanding all of the details I just move instinctively, as a mother, and immediately dial his cell number, knowing exactly what I must say.

He picks up the call after the first ring and says," Hi Mom," with such deep shame and sadness in his voice.

I say with as much kindness and support as I can muster, "What do you need, Sweetie? What do you need?"

Jake bursts into tears and says, "I need you to tell me that this is going to be alright."

"It'll be alright, Sweetie. We'll get through this," I say, barely containing my own emotions, and then I ask, "Can I come and get you now?"

He says, "Yes."

I grab my coat and boots, jump into my Jeep and drive the longest hour of my life, desperate to get to Jake, and just hold him and have him know that I will do whatever it takes to support him through this crisis. My suspicions have been correct; he hasn't been attending classes. He has been sleeping through the day and staying up all night, online, playing video games and chatting with his social connections, just as he had been doing at home this past summer. He hasn't had a meal plan, so he was surviving on what little food I was providing, and a few pizzas that he'd ordered. He's been living a secret life and lying to us for the past two months. All kinds of emotions are running through my mind as I begin to unravel what has transpired. A part of me is angry; I am sad, and I am disappointed. But an even bigger part of me is terrified. I am now worried that I won't get to Jake on time. I am deeply concerned that now that the truth is out, he won't be able to physically face me, that the shame will overcome him. I am scared for his life. No mother ever wants to experience this terrifying, uncontrollable kind of fear. I can't call him; I won't drive and talk on my phone. I need to arrive safely. All I can do is pray and have faith that I will get to him on time.

A very long hour later I arrive at Jake's residence and he answers the door. He looks shattered and defeated. He is so thin, so pale, his eyes are dilated, and he is shaking. I am quickly scanning him as though we've been separated for months; truly seeing him, as though for the very first time. This is not the vibrant little boy I raised; this person standing before me is a broken, sad soul of a young man. My heart is aching. He looks like an addict, and as I am thinking about this, I now recognize that he may be an addict; perhaps addicted to video gaming. We hug, and we cry. We stand there for what feels like an eternity, embraced in this moment of defeat and sanctuary. Here in my arms is my young son in great need of my help and my unconditional love. He is filled with shame and fear, and in his fragile state I am reminded that he is still a mere child inside. Adulthood is a very new experience for him, and one that he has very little experience from which to draw. I am the experienced and seasoned adult in this moment. And although I am so afraid of saying or doing the wrong thing, overcoming trauma and obstacles is a place of familiarity for me. I know that we can get through this and come out the other side triumphant. It will take an enormous amount of courage and inner strength from both of us, and I need to be a pillar on which Jake can lean, and from which he can push off from. The first step exists just outside of these walls. We decide to get out of Jake's residence, a house filled with the energy of fear, remorse, and despair. We drive to the mall just down the street for a bite to eat, and to talk. I just want to feed my son until he feels emotionally and physically full, and to keep telling him that everything is going to be fine.

~~~~~~

As my brain is unravelling and trying to make sense of the fallout from this situation, I start to feel the betrayal of all of Jake's lies and for a brief moment I allow myself to go to this place. I tell Jake, angrily that he's cost us his year's Registered Education Savings Plan funds, and he's foolishly sacrificed co-op in his program. He cannot fail or drop out of any courses and still maintain the co-op portion of his program, which means that he may now fall back to a degree curriculum that will not include any work placements. I am sorry as soon as I say it. Jake is angry at my reaction and tells me so. He is right. This is not about money or betrayal, this is about the raw emotional state of my son, and I quickly check my emotions and re-focus back to one of complete support. I tell myself I will make a phone call later at home and sort out the financial mess, and if money isn't recoverable, then it will just have to be okay. We eat and then we talk, and we walk, and Jake tells me in more detail how he has managed to live in residence, and not attend a single class or lecture, dodging the system for weeks. He confesses to the many hours of video gaming and online chat rooms he spent the dark hours in, explaining that it became his only escape from his anxiety, his guilt, and his very low feelings about himself. It was the only time that he didn't have to think about the mess he was creating. He confessed that he felt sick lying to me, and that he knew that I'd always told him that he could come to me with any problem and that I'd always have his back, but that he also knew how much I hated lying, and he'd been doing nothing but lying to both himself and to his family. We talk about how this should be handled, and I make a temporary suggestion. I mention that there's a possibility he can return in second semester and perhaps not lose his entire year. I know that we have to take more time to really sort all of this mess out. I am feeling numb and tired and need to take a break from all of the talking. I need time to think and to plan how to move forward.

We don't drive home, which is where I think that Jake should be. We don't move him out of residence, either. He has a few more days until he has to leave university behind for this semester. Jake had already made arrangements to spend the weekend with his brother in Toronto. Again, I am in a very uncomfortable position. It's a challenge deciding whether to assert my authority as a parent and have Jake come home for the weekend or allow him to make his own adult decision about where he feels he needs to be. We talk it through. I know that Jake has a lot of love and support from his brother, and he will be in a safe and supervised place with him and Myles. I decide to go along with his plan and take him to Toronto. This will give me time on my own to create a meaningful plan and I can still keep in touch with Jake. He promises not to shut me out anymore. He wants to be able to tell his brother himself and asks me not to say anything. He also asks me not to tell his father, that he feels it should also come from him. He promises to send him an email later this evening.

Despite many text back and forth between us, with my urging, Jake fails to send any messages to his dad, and I am left feeling like I am living a lie with my husband by not telling him. I pretend like nothing new has occurred and spend a quiet evening at home with Brian. It's the end of a workweek and he is tired, so he doesn't notice anything out of the ordinary. I feel sick inside and wish it could be out in the open amongst us now, so that we can deal with it together. I eventually go to bed, angry and hurt that Jake has ignored me, again. He has not followed through with his promise and has left me in an uncomfortable predicament. I abhor lying and I do not like that I have been silenced because he hasn't followed through with his promise.

Chapter 15

It is the next morning before Brian gets an email, and his reaction is natural in the face of betrayal. He is angry. I am not surprised. He's not considering the emotional turmoil that Jake has been experiencing while living his double life; he only sees that Jake has lied. I understand. I experienced some of that, as well. He is also angry that I didn't tell him. I see that I have more than one fire to put out. He doesn't believe me when I tell him that I was unaware of the situation until yesterday, when I received Jake's email. He accuses me of covering for Jake. He has no idea how difficult it was not to tell him last night. Thankfully Jake has finally come clean with him. There's no way I could carry out that charade for weeks. Emotions between us are high, and this tension is not helping any of us. Our conversation becomes heated as Brian continues to feel angry and betrayed by Jake's actions and I become frustrated that he won't see it as a cry for help. I am eventually able to get the point across to him that this is not about us; this is about Jake, he is in crisis, and needs us. We somehow manage to find a common ground from which to move forward and handle this situation with more grace. We spend the rest of the weekend conversing and sorting out all of our emotions and coming up with some sort of plan. I know that Jake will need a lot of empathy and understanding, and strength and firmness to lean on. Parenting our sons, I have always been the rule maker, the planner, the glue that holds the family structure together. Brian is a loving father, but he tends to be less involved with emotional issues. He believes I have a better handle on this and trusts my judgement. It will be me who walks Jake through the healing process, and Brian will support me in this endeavor. I have a lot to shoulder but am relieved to know that Brian and I are now on the same page.

Jake surprises me by confessing at the end of the weekend that he has still not told his brother of his sudden departure from university life. He says he feels too much shame and doesn't want to disappoint Nick. I feel relieved that he at least felt comfortable enough to tell me but am surprised that he doesn't think his brother can handle the truth. I tell him that he has to face this one person at a time and that even if it's tough to tell Nick, he will feel a sense of relief and the freedom to move forward when he does confess. I firmly tell Jake that he needs to break it to his brother or that I will be the one to tell him. I truly believe that revealing the truth will help Jake to start to heal from this emotional turmoil, and I refuse to cover up for him.

Jake finally relents and tells his brother what has transpired in his life over the past two months. And he finds, surprisingly, that Nick is more than supportive; he is an enormous comfort and offers to do whatever Jake needs to help him get back on track. Jake is moved to tears by Nick's support. And I am completely relieved. I am no longer alone with the secret. The whole family knows, and we are a united force ready to get behind Jake.

Jake and I have another discussion; this one about what will transpire once he returns home early in the week. I have failed Jake by ignoring key signs that he was in trouble. It's key for me to keep my eyes wide open to every clue that something may be amiss. There is an expression that "sometimes you have to be cruel to be kind" and although I believe that cruel is perhaps a little harsh, I do know that I must be solid in setting up some basic ground rules.

I demand that Jake remove the online interactive video game

from his computer that he's become so dependent upon. He agrees. Jake must get back on the day shift; no more staying up until the early morning hours and sleeping all day. Jake will be required to see our family doctor and get some much-needed counselling for his anxiety. I suggest bloodwork and a check-up be done, as Jake is severely underweight. He is 6'2" tall and now weighs in at only 127 lbs. He is clearly underweight and undernourished. He says yes to this rule, as well. He will have to do chores to help me around the house and look for a part-time job while he's home for the rest of this semester. He will also have to start eating healthy meals and getting outside for walks and attending fitness classes. He says that he's onboard and ready to commit to feeling better and creating some healthier habits. I insist that Jake consider returning to university for second semester, which will begin in the New Year. I suggest a lighter schedule, not a full-time student workload. I am afraid that if he takes more time off, he will lose momentum and perhaps not want to return to school at all. He has told me that he still wants to get his degree and continue to attend Guelph U so I want to encourage him to stay the course, so to speak. Had he told me that university just wasn't for him and that he didn't want to stay in his program, we would have looked at other options.

~~~~~~

Two days later I help Jake pack up and move out of his residence. Inside, the energy in the townhouse feels heavy, sad. Although it's situated in a quiet, secluded space, it feels eerily silent, more like a dead zone. Jake feels uncomfortable being there, and so do I. We pack quickly, and I secretly hope that when he returns for second semester that this place is no longer available for him to live in. I feel there are way too many triggers here, and it doesn't provide Jake with an atmosphere conducive to any kind of social life outside. We drive home to start the next chapter.

Jake starts to eat more healthily, and he works hard to get

back to a daytime schedule. This takes a little time and he suffers with headaches as the days wear on and his fatigue hits. For months he has been sleeping all day, and it's quite an adjustment to make his body return to wakefulness during this time. It's like returning from a long trip where the time change is twelve hours ahead and he's fighting extreme jet lag. We have to be patient with this. He starts helping with chores around the house, and I take him with me on errands into town. I am afraid to leave him alone, and I white-knuckle through each day, terrified of a relapse. Jake talks about the difficulty of not being able to play video games and recognizes that he is going through a withdrawal process. I am relieved that he is able to share his feelings after hiding them from me for so long.

While we are in town, I suggest that Jake pick up some job applications and start applying for a part-time job to give him more purpose for waking up in the mornings. Jake calls his boss from the pub he was working at during the summer, and he decides to give Jake some weekend hours, as dictated by how busy the restaurant is. Thankfully Jake has a good work ethic, and his boss is delighted to be able to add him back to the staff.

Two weeks later I am able to get an appointment for Jake to see our family doctor. The doctor is shocked at his condition, and upon hearing his story begins a full health check, orders blood work, and agrees that there is justification for concern. Jake is so thin that his bones are showing, and it sets off alarm bells for the doctor. He also suggests to us that Jake has Attention Deficit Disorder, and that it is the reason that he couldn't cope with school and all of its responsibilities, and why he ultimately checked out. Jake and I immediately disagree. Sure, Jake is a bit of a twitchy individual who cannot sit still; even in a state of rest, Jake's body will be in constant subtle motion. He also struggles to organize school and tasks at home. But I wasn't seeing the connection between Jake's need to fidget and his all-nighters with gaming as a sign of ADD. And when the doctor recommended prescribing a drug to treat Jake for ADD, I was even less enthused with what seemed to be a rather hasty diagnosis. Jake has never been good with medication, and easily breaks out in hives or a skin rash after administration. And as a holistic health practitioner, my feeling is that we could consider a more natural method of treatment, if that were necessary. But I am not even ready to accept the diagnosis. Am I being naïve, am I in denial? We do agree that Jake is suffering with anxiety. We say no to medication for this, also. Jake and I both concur that counselling would be the best option to begin to unravel the process of his dilemma.

So, our doctor agrees to put into place a counsellor who would be suitable and available to start seeing Jake as soon as possible. But he also wants Jake to follow up in a couple of weeks to see how he is doing and to discuss medication again, if there is no improvement. This seems fair.

On the drive home from the doctor's office Jake tells me that he is happy he is not going to have to take any prescription drugs. He is adamant that pharmaceuticals are not an option. We're on the same page and this is good. We are already being proactive with some healthy steps by adding nutritional food and exercise to Jake's daily regime, and there is still more work to come.

Chapter 16

A few years following Jake's illness and consequent recovery, using complementary medicine and a cleaner diet, I found myself more interested in the holistic health field. I eventually returned to school and learned the fascinating field of Iridology. Within the study of the iris, I also learned nutrition, allergy eliminations, the study of herbs and some energy medicine. By the time Nick and Jake were both attending school, full time, I had set up my holistic health business with a clinic in our home. This gave me the flexibility to create my own hours so that I could balance work with motherhood. It was a great fit for me and my family, and I enjoyed my work immensely.

The elementary school experience wasn't easy for Jake, and he often complained of his dislike of it. Despite this, he did manage to complete the curriculum with decent grades. By Grade Seven Jake was ready for placement in a fully integrated gifted program with students of like mind and intelligence. Initially he found it far better to be in this setting, as he felt he was finally a part of a tight group. Previous to this Jake had found himself feeling isolated in mainstream classes, and now he had found peers that he could relate to. However, the workload became intolerable for him, and he struggled to keep up. His biggest frustration with this specialized program was the assumption that if one is gifted, then it is assumed that they can handle a greater amount of work. So, added to the enhanced curriculum was a yearlong independent study unit. This was a massive project that was to be accomplished outside of the classroom. He found it ridiculous and highly unnecessary. And to make matters worse, Jake struggled with school testing. This had been an ongoing theme in his earlier grades that was still left unresolved. As his Grade Seven teacher described it, Jake knew the work, and if she asked him to answer questions, Jake had no difficulties. But once forced to sit down with paper and pen and asked to write down the answers within a limited time frame, it was as if he froze with anxiety. His brain shut down and he was unable to proceed with the test. The teacher suggested that she split Jake's test up so that he could write half of it in the morning and the second half in the afternoon, as she agreed it seemed it was an anxiety related issue. She proceeded with the plan. This did help and lessened the stress for both Jake and his educator.

But the heavy workload continued, and although Jake was making good grades, he was feeling enormous pressure and immense unhappiness in the program. He was being challenged but he felt like it was all work and there was never any time for play or to recharge; he was being pushed beyond his emotional capability. Jake then began to find the middle school years socially difficult. He experienced a period of being ostracized. This is a time of struggle for many students; puberty has a cruel way of making one look and feel awkward. And if a child is different, in any way, it is magnified. Jake's saving grace was his solid relationship with his brother, and they were still able to spend some quality time together outside of school. But it was apparently not enough. I would learn later that Jake's sense of isolation at school was a huge issue, but one that Jake was hiding well. I had no idea until much later just how sad and alone he'd been feeling at school.

Just five weeks shy of the completion of Grade Eight and

middle school graduation, Jake became extremely ill. He would not return to school, nor would he be present at his graduation ceremony to receive the Media Award that he'd won. Jake was very sad about this. Months would unfold, with Jake fighting to recover from chronic fatigue, nausea, headaches, muscle cramps, and chest pains, before the idea of attending full time school would again be a reality.

At the early onset of this mysterious illness, weeks would pass with Jake only waking briefly to sip a vitamin drink packed with electrolytes, and to get to the bathroom with the use of a walker. He had the strength of a sickly newborn, and as time progressed he would need assistance with bathing and dressing. Visits to medical specialists and the emergency room in the hospital, blood tests, intravenous liquid fuel to treat dehydration and raise his blood pressure, x-rays, ultra-sounds and neuromuscular probing all became a part of our new normal. It was like we'd gone back in time again. As had occurred thirteen years earlier with Jake's mysterious digestive ailment, the doctors once again scratched their heads for lack of a diagnosis. No one knew what was making him so debilitated or how to make him well again. At first it was an absolutely frightening experience for our family. The onset was so acute. The lingering symptoms with no answers from the medical field for weeks had us all worried that Jake might never fully recover. Brian and I played tag with watching and caring for Jake, as we never wanted him to be left alone. There were many times that I would place my face close to Jake's to hear if he was still breathing and still alive, as he lay sleeping, seemingly lifeless. He was like a little baby bird, who when I came by with a drink and brought a straw close to his lips, he would open his mouth and take a sip or two, never opening his eyes, and instantly drift back into a deep sleep.

As the months passed and it was clear that Jake wasn't suffering from anything life-threatening, our family accepted that we needed to assist Jake in getting nutrition and food into his system. We continued to look for an answer. But we didn't panic anymore. Jake was eventually able to be awake for one meal a day, and he no longer required the walker to get to the bathroom. And at times he was alert long enough to do a limited amount of school work. That was arranged and set up at home through the secondary school guidance department, the head of guidance being one of immense support through this trying time. But Jake continued to suffer with muscle pain, nausea, and chest pains. Thankfully, the extreme fatigue allowed him to sleep through much of the discomfort. Doctor visits were trying, as I was forced to wake, bathe and dress Jake for his appointments. He would sleep in the car on the way there and back, and sometimes would be asleep on the examining table while waiting to see the doctor, or while having a blood test done. It was heartbreaking to watch him lose so much weight, to see him so placid, and so unwell. He was once my lively teenager, wiggling, squirming, and always active. Now he barely had the strength to thrive.

As had happened when Jake was sick, as a baby, I began to lose faith in the medical field's ability to help him. I was not angry about it; I had respect for this science and understood that for a doctor to treat Jake, they would require a diagnosis, but all test results were coming up empty. We were told that it must be a virus, and that identifying which virus it was would be like "looking for a needle in a haystack." It was suggested that we continue to keep doing what we were doing and ride it out until Jake's body recovered on its own. But eleven months had passed, and Jake was six feet tall and now weighed just 125 pounds; I could see his ribs sticking out on the front and back of his body; his face was gaunt, and he could barely walk more than a few feet without getting fatigued and needing to lie back down. He was a teenager who should have been eating me out of house and home and constantly gaining weight. I couldn't continue to watch him wither away, and I feared that his muscles would eventually atrophy from lack of movement, and that he'd never recover completely. He'd already lost much of his first year of secondary school, barely getting through the workbook assignments, and I didn't want him to fall behind another year. I was beginning to see a pattern with Jake, both with school and with his health, and it appeared that traditional methods didn't offer enough answers or solutions to meet his needs. I refused to allow Jake, once again, to be left to fall through the abyss of an imperfect system. So, I began to research an alternative method for gaining back Jake's health and vitality. We would, once again, simply attack this from a different direction.

As a holistic health practitioner, I had a large network of colleagues with whom I could speak. At the last specialist appointment, I had learned that Jake's vitamin D levels were extremely low, and he was already taking a course of 5,000 units a day. So, I looked at the idea that Jake's tissues may be lacking other minerals. It was suggested to me by a natural health practitioner I had spoken with, that I pick up tissue salts specific to a chronic fatigue ailment. The pediatrician overseeing Jake's care was fully supportive of this action. I began to see some improvements, and Jake became more alert and he was able to eat more. This new alertness seemed quite incredible to both Jake and I. He described them as a sort of magic pill; they provided the progress he was looking for. Healing requires energy, building muscles requires energy, even thinking requires energy. Since Jake had no energy, prior to this, he could barely think about recovery. Tissue salts provided the vitality he needed for his body to begin to mend itself. Week by week Jake gained more strength making the salts act as an accelerator for recovering faster.

Once Jake had the strength to remain awake for longer periods in the day I took the advice of another practitioner and got Jake to a traditional Chinese medicine doctor to see if acupuncture might help. Following the initial consultation, I felt hopeful that this was the right direction to take. After spending a lengthy period of time in a medical dead end, it was apparent that Jake would, once again, require a professional who would guide his recovery with non-traditional methods. Moving forward I realized that formulating a plan that would include both traditional and complementary approaches from the onset of any health issue Jake may contract in the future, would both enhance and speed up the process of his recovery.

Acupuncture and Chinese herbs were the answer to Jake's road back to wellness, and his response to this treatment was fast and effective. Jake liked the doctor and found him to be gentle and supportive through treatment. Spring and summer that year was spent with Jake drinking a daily concoction of a ghastly-smelling and-tasting mixture of herbal remedies. Two days a week he laid on a table with several acupuncture needles poking into the surface of his skin. The sensation of the needles was different each time. Jake said that they sometimes tingled, sometimes itched, and at times the tingling would run up the length of his limb. There were times the needles created a very heavy sensation and at other times they created intense heat. His appetite soon improved; he needed less sleep; the strength in his muscles started to slowly improve, and the headaches and chest pains disappeared. Jake was gaining weight, but he was still quite weak by any standard for a normal teenager. He could walk and move around a little more, but when he sat down he couldn't hold his upper body up for even a short period of time.

I later asked Jake if he was ever concerned that he would never feel better. He told me that he wasn't worried that his body wouldn't recover. If anything, he knew when it was recovering. He was aware of when his body was no longer on a downhill battle, and recognized the point when things appeared to be going uphill, in his recovery.

By the end of July Jake needed to consider starting his

first full year of secondary school, but he would need to first begin a tough regimen with a physiotherapist to build back complete strength in his core, his legs and arms, so that he could manage carrying a backpack full of books and then sitting through classes. This was where the real battle took place in his recovery. The question, for Jake was whether or not he wanted to return to school. Did he want to deal with the "same crap" he'd left behind, before he became ill? Would anything be any different once he was healthy? The illness, for Jake, had created a bubble of protectiveness from school pressure and the bullying. He eventually told himself that if he wanted to live in reality, he'd have to return to school. He knew he couldn't hide from it forever, and so he chose to heal. He said he healed because living is a better option than dying, and he realized it was his decision to make.

Jake began a physiotherapy program to strengthen his muscles. He described this time as one in "auto-pilot". He wasn't fond of the exercises he was required to do, both during physio and at home. But he needed to be strong and went through the motions to get through the many physical tasks.

Re-entry to school in the fall was exciting for Jake. After a long haul, wasting away in his bedroom, he was anxious to get back to living. He had felt isolated in the recovery and needed to have regular social contact again with his friends. He also had a lot of catching up to do and set an ambitious goal to complete secondary school in the remaining three years. He deserved to walk across the stage to receive his graduation diploma along with his peers. He entered the gifted program again, with the understanding that if it became too much pressure, he could pull out and continue with a regular curriculum. His program was modified, allowing Jake to write tests in a separate, quieter space, and received extra time to complete his exams. This helped enormously, and as a result, Jake's confidence in his ability rose. He made friends with more ease and found himself a circle of good people to hang with, at first the students from his enhanced classes, and then later on he'd also find friendship amongst his art class peers. Jake participated with the tennis team and then the table tennis group at school. Outside of school, he was involved in an archery club and continued to play recreational tennis and to snowboard. Life seemed pretty normal and Jake felt really happy again. He found that keeping up with school assignments was a little easier now. He had to work harder to get through homework, and still resented the extra time that it took.

But he had a whole new appreciation for education. During that year of illness, Jake realized the importance of having a classroom setting, peer discussion, and a teacher for guidance, especially while he was working within the vacuum of his isolated bedroom setting with just his computer. Doing all of his school work from home actually proved to be a blessing in disguise. I felt enormous relief; all of those years of struggle helping Jake to find his comfort zone in an environment where he felt quite out of his element had finally paid off. Jake was now learning how to work within his limitations, and without entering a school environment, and find a way to get through it.

Chapter 17

    Jake is adjusting well, being away from university and now home again. He is taking daily walks and has started participating in my fitness classes, working with my personal trainer. He finds this is really helping to lift him out of the fog he's been in and to adjust back to a daytime schedule.

A week later Jake meets for the first time with his counsellor, a local social worker, and with whom Jake immediately feels comfortable. We are fortunate that we could skip the waiting list and that Jake now has the help of a therapist. Jake had many concerns about counselling before entering into it, and he is quite nervous. He mentioned to me earlier that he didn't know how he would talk or what kinds of things he should discuss. I explained that the therapist would know how to prompt Jake with questions to get a discussion started. I had also had an opportunity to speak with the counsellor, on the phone and made him aware of the events that led up to Jake needing to see him, before the first session began. After we spoke, I felt confident that Jake would open up under the counsellor's guidance.

But I have another concern, and I will have to learn to let it go and trust in the process. As Jake is an adult I will not be privy to what is discussed during their time together, unless he is willing to share it. I don't want him to feel that he has to share; I want to give him the space to work it out independently. However, I also know that Jake has been lying to himself and to me for the past many months, and I do have concerns about how honest he will be with the counsellor. Until he recognizes just how deeply serious this ordeal is, he may have a tendency to downplay it. This will be the first litmus test, a testament to Jake's desire to get better, to get truly healthier at an emotional level. I am comforted that Jake has someone objective to share his feelings with, and I am relieved when Jake comes out of the first hour saying that it was good to see someone and easy to talk to his new therapist. He said that once he got started, he talked and talked and talked until time was up. He tells me that he has also been given an exercise by the counsellor to do before his next session in a week's time.

Jake and I start spending a lot of time together, which allows us to talk a lot about what had transpired for us in the last several months. We have many discussions about the details of Jake's living environment while he was at university, how he managed to remain holed up in his dorm room and under the radar for so long, and about his unrelenting draw to video gaming, which was spending all of his waking hours. It becomes quite apparent that he hadn't stopped the video gaming habit since he'd been home. Although I had worked to put him back on a daytime schedule at home, at the end of August, once he got back to university and had the freedom to make his own choices, he was powerfully drawn back to gaming. He felt afraid and alone, back at school. He immediately got back on line and started pulling all-nighters, explaining that being alone with himself and his overactive brain was almost painful, from which gaming was an easy escape. He didn't have to think about anything but the game and getting to the next level. He felt this gave him purpose, but what it was giving him was an escape from reality. It was a virtual world that didn't in any way help him meet his goals in life. The more we talk, the more Jake recognizes that gaming provides a chemical high and an escape that he can't seem to get anywhere else. And he's also built what he considers some very meaningful friendships in the online world. It has been his nocturnal, virtual social life. I feel so sad knowing Jake has been living in such a sad, isolated environment, cut off from the day to day activities and routine of university life. It pains me to know that he was suffering, and he felt the only way to cope was to hide out, in the middle of the night, in a virtual world. To know that he wasn't taking care of his basic needs, not grooming and barely eating, just breaks my heart. But I also understand why he felt the need to escape, and it's apparent that he wanted to find a way that worked for him, at the time. He needed to go to this low, dark period, to check out of what seemed like a time filled with too much pressure. It was providing him with temporary relief, and that's about all that he could manage at the time.

Jake has always loved people, especially being around people older than him, but he also has a good network of friends from secondary school that he has maintained. I had hoped he would stay in touch with them during university. But he slowly let these friendships die off, and his social interaction was being replaced with his video world. Jake is a talker and loves lengthy conversations, but because he hadn't been attending classes, he'd lost touch with face-to-face interactions. Both at home during the summer and while he was away at school, he had become totally immersed in a dark lifestyle. Not drinking, not drugs, not promiscuous sex or crime. Jake was caught up in the highly destructive (to him) world of interactive video gaming. He was barely eating. He was disengaged from personal contact with others. He had stopped grooming himself. He was completely withdrawn from university life. He was lying, and he was hiding. Jake's skin had broken out in numerous blemishes; his hair had become perpetually greasy. He was grossly underweight; his hands shook; and his eyes were dilated, and if I didn't know any better I would have guessed that he was a drug user. He had looked and behaved similar to a substance abuse addict. That is the young man I brought home from a dorm room; this is the person I am nurturing back to health. And it is terrifying to think how easily Jake can be pulled back into such a sad and wasteful place.

Addiction is very familiar to me. My father was an alcoholic and he didn't have the inner strength or conviction to fight the addiction and remain sober; no amount of begging and pleading from my mother, no amount of tears and disappointment in the eyes of me or my brothers could make him stop drinking. I knew the pull; I knew how seductive the obsessive world of addiction was. It's random, it doesn't discriminate. It waits, and it haunts. It draws one in, especially during low periods, weak moments, and down times. I know I have my work cut out for me, with Jake, and I need to elicit as much help in supporting him as I possibly can. I am not in a position to judge or label Jake an addict, but I do know that I can keep communication open and we can discuss healthier choices for dealing with stressful times. The more I learn about Jake's decline, the more I realize that this is not something I can manage with him, on my own. I need back up.

~~~~~~

In early December Jake re-visits our family doctor and gets results from his blood work. Everything is good, apart from his vitamin D levels. Jake has always struggled with keeping these numbers up, so it comes as no surprise, especially when he had previously been sleeping during the day, for months, and understanding that vitamin D is derived from the sun. He immediately starts taking a supplement of 2,000 units daily. In the early evening I receive a text from my sister-in-law, who lives on the west coast, to tell me that my mom has had a bad fall and has entered hospital. A scan revealed that a post-stroke seizure created the fall. This is very upsetting, as my Mom has already experienced physical and cognitive decline from the original stroke, and this will only make matters worse. She cannot live safely on her own anymore. This is an additional worry for me. I now have the added burden of helping to arrange future care options for my mom. The timing is poor, but we can't predict when life's challenges will fall on our lap. The health and well-being of my mother is as vital as the health of my son, but I barely have the strength to shoulder the extra weight of this responsibility. I feel terribly helpless that I am unable to leave Ontario and fly to her bedside to do more, but I am comforted in knowing that my brother and sister-in-law are handling the situation, from the west coast, the best they can.

At this time Jake also receives news back from the university that his return for semester two in January has been accepted. He will be able to take the minimum of three courses that will enable him to return to residence. Jake appears to be happy about the news and agrees that having a lighter course load will help him to handle school and classes with more ease.

It is now time to choose his courses, but as we talk about his choices I get a strange sense that something isn't quite right with regard to his first-year credits. Having pertinent information withheld by Jake has been a continuing theme, and I can't ignore my maternal intuition. The sticky part is that once your child attains the age of eighteen, a parent is no longer privy to end-of-semester, or end-of-year school reports informing you as to how your son or daughter is managing with his or her grades. I know I have no legal rights to see his grades from year one. However, in light of the months of deception, I exercise my authority this time, and insist that Jake show me his results from first year. At first Jake tells me that he passed all of his courses. But I am not buying it. I press for more honesty and Jake finally agrees to show me his school records, online. My instincts prove to be correct. Not only has he failed an important computer math credit, but he has also failed an elective course. And his grades are definitely not up to his potential in some of his courses. I start to see that year one was a bigger disaster than I had been led to believe. The math class was essential for Jake to advance to year two. He explains that it was much more challenging than he had anticipated. I ask if he had requested any help with this. He had not. I ask how he could have failed something as easy as the elective credit. Jake tells me he stopped attending classes and had convinced himself that he could still pass by catching up through online reading. It was a bad idea and he now knows it. I am suddenly filled with flashbacks of those times in first year, during his second semester, when I would drive to visit Jake or pick him up from residence in mid-afternoon. I'd text and get no answers, and then when I finally went inside and knocked on his door, I'd discover that he was often still asleep in his very dark room. He'd crawl out of bed still wearing his clothes. His hair was greasy and his body odour stank. It is apparent only now that Jake's issues with university had started back then; he was already pulling all-nighters in year one. The many funny stories he told of hanging out in the hallways with other students and doing his homework were manufactured. This lie has been a manipulation that Jake has managed to pull off for a very long time, and I fear that his dishonesty is now habitual, and may take some time and diligence to break. There is much more work to do and I feel overwhelmed by it.

It now occurs to me that without that essential math class, Jake may never get back into the co-op program. I feel sick inside. I missed some significant clues and I didn't see through his lying. I trusted. I believed he could manage. I was wrong, and I feel somehow responsible. I should have known, as a mother, that Jake was not ready for the responsibility of university. How could I not know this? He is my son. I am concerned that he may feel pushed to do school when it's not really something he wants or can do. So, I ask him to get really honest; I want to know if getting his degree is still something he wishes to do. I ask if he still wants to return to the co-op program. Jake assures me that this is what he wants. He then chooses his credits for next semester and continues a forward motion towards his education goals.

The pub calls Jake in for part-time shifts more regularly. Jake is so happy to be back in the restaurant with people he loves and where he is recognized as a great worker and a fun staff member. I am relieved for him to be making social connections again, and for him to have some purpose. This job may be a confidence booster. I start to relax, but only a little.

Chapter 18

    I have always been an empathic person, and as a result I have a keen awareness of other people's emotions, without them expressing them to me in words or actions. I can be standing next to a stranger and feel the energy around them, whether it is tension or deep pain, even if we don't speak a word to each other. I think we all have the ability to read people in this way, if we pay close attention. The best example I can give is this: you're in a room with your friend or significant other, and you feel like they might be upset with you. Something just doesn't feel right. You ask them if they are okay, and they tell you that they are. But, somehow you just sense that they are not. You can't put a finger on it, but you just have this knowing. And later on, you learn that they were upset, but they were just not willing to share it with you. You were right. Through these kinds of observation, I have learned that we all emit energy, good or bad, hot or cold, happy or angry. Just as I am often aware of other people's energy, I am also cognizant of the energy that I am putting out there. I am a strong believer that what you send out will always come back to you, mirrored. And for me personally, I have come to realize that when I am operating from a place of integrity and when I behave with the best and most loving intentions, then my energy is great. And when I slip up and come from a place of selfishness or self-righteousness, then my energy is low and dark. We all have those moments when the scales tip to one extreme or the other. Sometimes I can get so anxious, sad, or frustrated that my energy feels almost depleted, while other times I am so elated and joyful that my energy is running high and on full throttle. My goal is to always strive to get to that place where I feel a sense of calm, peace, and satisfaction, but it can take a few steps to arrive there, and sometimes a little longer than I'd like it to take. It takes practice to find the right balance. In a crisis, when emotions can run high and things can get out of control pretty quickly, initially I don't deny myself from feeling whatever feelings arise. I give myself permission to have a bit of a pity party. I cry, scream, or whine, or I journal all of my negative emotions, writing and getting everything off my chest until it's all out there, on paper. And then eventually I make myself stop and switch gears, and I begin the work of centering and grounding myself again. I start to remember all that I have, all that I am blessed with and grateful for, and I either list it in my head or I write it down. I do this for as long as it takes, until I return to a place of love. Instead of shaking my fist at the universe and asking why, I then say thank you. During those times that it doesn't work, and I can't seem to pull out of the funk, I call on someone else to support me through it, to remember for me, and steer me in a more positive direction. Thoughtful and caring friends and family members can be a great source for lifting me up when my inner strength is depleted. Spiritual leaders, counselors, and energy workers can also help. I have sought assistance from all of the above at various times in my life. I can't say what's best for others, but this is what works for me. I gauge what is needed as I am presented with life's adversity. I try to remain grounded and solid, but I am at peace when I fall apart and need to ask for help; there is strength in both.

~~~~~~

In December I receive a call from Myles; she is distraught and needs comfort. She tells me that she and Nick are splitting up. Just as Jake's email in November takes me off guard, this information strikes me like a bat to the side of the head. I didn't see this coming and I am heartbroken for both of them.

I can't take sides. I can't stop the break-up. But I can sit with each of them individually and hear each side, and so I do. A long story unravels, and I see that this relationship was a train wreck waiting to happen. Neither of them had come forward or asked for help with their relationship issues, and Nick especially didn't feel that he could have burdened me with them. I feel a failure as a mother, once again, for not realizing that he was feeling troubled and needed me. And I start to now understand his anger and his pulling away from me for the past many months. Nick has always seemed so fiercely independent, which has left me with a false sense of security. I assumed he wouldn't need me so much. I have let him down, too. I feel emotionally-beaten and overpowered, like my life is moving down a steep slope and I can't stop the momentum. This break-up just can't be happening. But it is, and I need to be strong, really strong. I can't waste time beating myself up for not seeing this coming and offering support to Nick sooner. I have to pick myself up and push my way through. Both Nick and Jake need my strength and understanding now, and that is where my loyalties must land.

I tell Nick that I understand how things went wrong, and how sorry he felt he couldn't speak with me about it. He must have felt alone in his pain. This evening I let him talk as much as he needs to and for as long as he needs to. It is as though a dam had broken to let the water burst through. Nick has so much to say, and his talking unravels months of repressed emotion. This disclosure, in a sense, starts some release of the anger that he'd directed at me a year ago, and suddenly instead of shutting me out, as he had, he is welcoming me back into his life. Even though I adore Myles and her family, and it will be painful to say good-bye, Nick's well-being and my kinship with him is far more important. We have some healing of our own to do in repairing our broken relationship.

Jake continues with weekly counselling, continues to exercise and eat well, and has gained back a lot of the weight he'd lost while at school. Things look positive, although for me there seems to be a gnawing fear close to the surface. I push it down, and replace with it happier thoughts, planning a nice

Christmas break.

Nick comes home for Christmas without Myles. I feel my own sadness and loss in not having her here with us, but I understand that being single again is what is best for Nick now. I will take the time needed to grieve, but not while Nick is around. I deal with my disappointment in private.

~~~~~~

On Christmas day we have a fabulously-relaxed morning with our gift exchange, followed by a home-cooked brunch. We remain home for the day, and Brian prepares us a beautiful roast beef dinner and an evening of board games and cards. I know it may sound old-fashioned and corny, but for me, there is no better time than time with my family, playing and having fun.

Boxing Day brings enough snow in the area for snowboarding at the local resort, and nothing could make Jake happier! He and Nick get up and hit the slopes early with plans to board all day. They tell me via text message that the conditions are great and there is hardly anyone else at the resort, so the guys are able to enjoy short line-ups on the lifts. They return home later that afternoon exhilarated that they'd gotten in about forty great runs. I imagine this day of free time to play was cathartic for them, each in his own way.

Nick returns to the city the next day, and Jake has friends from out of town arriving for a visit. His long-time online friend, Eren, is visiting from the U.K., along with his long-distance girlfriend Robyn, who is from the New Jersey. They have both driven to our home in Canada to stay for a few days. Jake and Eren haven't seen each other since their trip to Japan. They have a great time together; Jake takes them snowboarding and into Toronto, and they spend New Year's Eve together in our home, while Brian and I attend my cousin's wedding and stay overnight in a hotel. It's a fun way to end the last part of 2014. I say a prayer of gratitude for all of the many blessings I have received and ask for continued support for myself and my family in the New Year. Jake has worked hard with his counsellor. He has shown that he wants to return to school and work towards getting his degree, and I tell myself that the plans we have implemented thus far should flow with ease. I recall having this same feeling when we launched Jake on his first year of university and am reminded at just how wrong I could have been. I know now to proceed, with caution.

Chapter 19

Jake shares his newest plan for university with me. It's one that he worked out with the counselor at his last session. First, he is going to re-take the first-year math class that is required for his software engineering program. And second, he will take two electives, one to make up for the elective he also failed, and one as an extra to take the pressure off future course loads. This plan Jake and I agreed on beforehand, and I am very comfortable with it. Jake tells me that the social worker, whom Jake has now met with a total of eight times in the past two months, agrees with his plan to incorporate some online video gaming time into his school schedule. He justifies this by explaining that because his eventual goal is to develop video games, it is vital that he spends time playing them. Alarm bells start screaming in my head as I hear this! Jake took an inordinate amount of time creating a schedule on paper, which outlines the free time that he will allow himself for gaming, and then presented it to his counselor for approval. He then tells me that this is their agreed-upon plan. I am completely uncomfortable with this and tell him so. Jake disagrees with me wholeheartedly and promises that he will stick to the schedule and practice the work hard to balance schoolwork with play. Every bone in my body tells me that Jake is either lying or that he has manipulated the counselor into believing that his emotional state is a whole lot better than I believe it is. I have seen Jake work really hard these past couple of months and I do see improvements. But I also know his vulnerability and his use of online gaming to escape stress, in my opinion it is a huge risk factor in his plan. I believe that sending Jake back into the same environment where he was anxious and left alone with his anxieties could trigger the exact same negative behaviour as before. But here's my dilemma; I am not legally allowed to discuss this with the social worker, because Jake is an adult, and I have no control over how he will behave once he leaves our home and goes back to residence. He is of age to make his own choices. But in my heart, I don't believe he has reached the emotional maturity level to make the best decisions for himself.

Herein lies the struggle, once again, of parenting an adult child versus parenting a child. I want to trust, and I want to give Jake the space to prove that he has learned enough skills to manage his time, but I am scared to death. And I can't force him to do what I think is best or what his counselor has approved of. I make a promise to myself to monitor it closely, and to jump in if I sense that trouble has prevailed; if there is even an inkling of suspicion I will be on Jake's doorstep. I cannot take the risk of Jake fading away again, unsupported and alone in his dorm room and worrying about how he will handle things a second time around. I do worry about the possibility of suicide. Jake knows I have his back, but will he be able to face the guilt and remorse a second time, and come clean with me if he's in trouble? This new plan of Jake's will require a huge leap of faith and a watchful eye by me.

Tonight, before bed, I write in my journal that I feel a nervous sadness. Jake will be returning to university in two more days, and although I'm happy for all of the work he's done to prepare, I will miss him, and I feel nervous for him. Again, the internal struggle – to let go or to be afraid that he's just not ready. Jake is behaving as though he's got this, that he can handle this newest challenge. I convince myself that letting go is the right thing to do. I am choosing to provide Jake the foothold I think he needs to maintain his confidence that he can manage this. I push hard to keep my fears locked down inside of me.

The following day Jake has his last counselling appointment and feels ready to return to school. We celebrate by going to the skydiving simulator, where Jake can take advantage of the gift certificate he received for Christmas. Skydiving is something Jake has spoken of for a long time. For a mother it's a scary thought to have your child fall from an airplane with a parachute, and I feel terrified at the prospect every time Jake mentions it. I decide to work on overcoming this fear, and today I take the time to speak with one of the representatives at the center. After our conversation I feel more educated about the preparation and safety aspects of a jump, and realize I am facing yet another lesson in learning to let go. I can't stop Jake from pursuing any of his goals and dreams as an adult, and I don't want to be the kind of mother who judges and criticizes his every choice. I want to be the kind of mother who trusts and supports him. With a little more education under my belt I think I can do this. I am secretly pleased that it will require many simulator runs and much preparation before Jake transitions from a simulator to an aircraft. In any case, it's way too expensive for him to afford as a student. So, I take comfort in knowing that it will be a few more years, at least, before I have to prove I trust this choice, as well.

Jake takes to the skydiving simulator runs like a pro, fearless, and full of excitement. He has success in his first rides, acquiring techniques that he will need in the process of reaching the highest level. I videotape and take photographs and celebrate along with him. I smile inside at the thought of this moment being another confidence-builder for a young man who has had such enormous struggles these past months. I am truly happy for Jake and for a moment can forget all of my fears about what is to come. I recognize the parallel in this moment - trusting and allowing Jake to take the plunge, in the air and in his life. He has to be free to make choices.

Semester two is about to begin. We pack up Jake's belongings and make our way back to the University of Guelph.

Jake returns to the same residence townhouse and to the same dorm room that he was in in his second year, and this leaves me unsettled. I am concerned that the isolation its location provides will be a detriment, and that Jake will experience the same anxieties. At home I can monitor Jake's actions and behaviour and intervene. Although he will be only an hour's drive away, it feels like much further, and my fear is overwhelming. I put my feelings aside and try to act as though I am confident in Jake's ability to manage. I don't want to fill him with doubt on the first day. We hug, and we say goodbye. I return home. I try to breathe and move forward, one step at a time.

Jake has shown a lot of maturity and tenacity making this transition back to school. He said he is nervous but ready. That's understandable. I hope that all the effort put in over the past two months will be enough to sustain Jake and get him back on the right track. I work hard to trust and have faith. I call upon my many angels to surround me with strength.

It's Monday, the first day of a new week and a new year, and it is Jake's first day of classes. I return to work after the Christmas break, looking to increase my clientele, a New Year's resolution most entrepreneurs embrace. I am busy in my clinic, but with every free moment I am thinking of Jake. At the end of his last class he sends me a text that says, "Survived day one." I am relieved. Jake is already reaching out via text, something he would rarely do in the previous semester. I see this as a good sign, but I still do not fully exhale.

I take a moment to be grateful that technology has reached the point where we can receive instant gratification in a message. It helps me to keep closer contact with Jake and at greater speed. But I also recognize the curse that it is. Jake can hide behind and pretend to be someone else behind a text. Today, texting outranks phone calls as the prevailing form of communication among young people. They see texting as a more efficient way to connect and get their message out, and they consider speaking on the telephone as an intrusive way to reach one another. And I am completely on board with this way of thinking. But texting also provides a place to hide from a difficult face-to-face conversation. I hope he is using this method of communication with absolute honesty and transparency.

I continue to communicate with Jake via text messaging a couple more times in the week; he tells me he saw the orthodontist and that his mouth is sore. I wonder if he is not eating again.

Breathe, Elaine, breathe and trust, runs through my head.

A parcel arrives at our home. It's the sweaters I ordered for Jake. I send a text and let Jake know they have arrived by courier and ask if he'd like me to bring them this weekend or wait until he's home on another weekend. He says to bring them sooner rather than later, as it's cold and windy walking to campus. Sounds good, sounds promising, but I have a gnawing feeling in my gut that I just can't shake, and the anticipation of seeing Jake in the flesh this weekend is rising like a thermostat turned up high inside of me. I refuse to be blindsided, once again. I have to see for myself and not naively pretend that Jake left for university with the best-laid plan and hasn't slipped up. That video gaming schedule he was going to implement quite frankly scares the hell out of me, and I can't get to the university fast enough.

~~~~~~~~~~~~~~~~~~~~~~~~~~~~~~~~~~~~~~~

 My husband and I agree to meet Jake at noon, on Saturday, at his dorm so that we can take him to lunch and have a visit. I am both nervous and so excited to see Jake. I want the lunch to be one of celebration. We knock on the door and Jake answers looking like absolute crap. The first thing I notice is the weight he's already lost in one week, and then I see his hands shaking and his pupils are dilated. He looks exhausted and spacey. I know in my heart and soul that he has returned to a place of darkness. He acts like everything's cool and that he is doing well. At first, I go along with it, trying not to come across overly-protective or paranoid. I understand that it will take kindness and compassion to draw the truth out of him. He's in a fragile state again. I ask myself how I could have thrown him back into school so soon. He's clearly not ready to manage being on his own yet.

Over lunch I start prodding and asking questions, gently at first, and then when I see that Jake just wants to continue the lie, I ask with more assertiveness. My husband isn't picking up on Jake's very obvious cues; he's choosing not to see and has distracted himself with the Australian Open tennis match playing on the restaurant's TV. Jake eventually confesses, and now I need back up.

"You can jump into the conversation anytime," I say to Brian.

"Why?" he asks. "All you're doing is grilling him."

I'm dumbfounded by his reply.

He doesn't realize that I already know the truth, and that Jake has just answered my queries honestly. Jake hadn't been to a single class this week. He's been up every night video gaming on the Internet, and then sleeping all day. I am annoyed with Brian and very concerned for Jake, but this restaurant is not the place to continue with the conversation. I tell Jake that he needs to come home for the weekend, and that we need to talk about it. We get up from the table when lunch is finished, and we head back to Jake's dorm room. As Jake gets out of the vehicle I tell him that we will wait in the car for him.

My husband is bewildered and asks me what is going on. He had no intention of returning home with Jake and finds this all very confusing. I am furious with him for refusing to look at what clearly needs to be seen, and I now let him know that Jake is right back where he started just a few months ago. I let him know that I am not happy with the fact that he is ignoring what is right in front of him. He clearly wants to believe that Jake is just fine. He begins to understand what is happening. My husband is again deeply disappointed and hurt by Jake's behaviour. I remind him, once again, that it's not about us; it's about Jake, and he clearly needs our help and support. It's far worse than I had imagined, and I'm not sure what to do next. I only know that I have to stay strong and I have to intervene again. Jake needs much more help.

It's a long, quiet drive home, each of us feeling our own individual pain; none of us knowing what to do about it. I feel like I have two people I need to help through this ordeal: first my son who is evidently troubled, and second, my husband who just doesn't understand the magnitude of Jake's apparent mental instability, or how he can be a help rather than a detriment. In my husband's defense he just doesn't want to see what's right in front of him; his son is in great need of empathy. This is not an area of which he has any real understanding of. He views this as naughty, defiant behaviour, while I am fully aware that to scold Jake would push him further down a rabbit hole of despair.

Chapter 20

Knowledge is the key to my understanding Jake's chronic pull towards the online world of video gaming. After last semester's crisis, I searched and found some good research and information about the concept of video gaming obsession and/or addiction. Jake's story is not unique, and gaming addiction is a serious issue. I admit that I danced around it before, and that I didn't take the steps required to deal with the issue diligently. With the recent discovery that he is still using gaming as a tool for avoiding school, it is even more important that I reconsider the addiction research data, get real about the problem, and provide the kind of support that Jake requires.

In my search for more information I have learned that seventy-two percent of teens play video games on their computer, game console, and/or portable device, such as their cell phones, and a larger number of these teens are boys. In the past twenty years, video gaming has evolved to increase the opportunity to interact and socialize with others while playing, without being in the same room as one's opponent. Of these "gamers", eighty-nine percent play with friends they know in person, fifty-four percent play with friends they have met online, and fifty-two percent interact with others who are not their friends.[1] I believe that in terms of these statistics,

Jake is a typical gamer.

More than half of teens have developed friendships online, which involves the use of both gaming and social media sites, and of these teens thirty-six percent of them say that they met their new friend(s) while engaged in video games. Twenty-three percent of teens report that they would give a new friend their gaming handle as contact information. Thirty-eight percent of these teens are boys, while only seven percent of teen girls would share the same information. Ninety-one percent of video-gaming boys say they play with others whom they are connected with through online multi-player networks like Xbox ™ Live or PlayStation ™ Network, and one third of boys say that they engage and play this way every day or almost every day.[1] Clearly, Jake falls into the former category: a daily user.

Fifty-nine percent of teens who play video games online with other gamers use a voice connection, much like speaking over a telephone, while they play. This then becomes a great vehicle for attracting friendship and social interaction. Of these, seventy-one percent are boys. And the older the teen, the more likely it is for them to connect with voice. A whopping seventy-five percent of boys aged 15-17 are using voice connection when they play online. [1] Jake has told me that he uses voice chat when playing with friends he knows, online, and otherwise uses a text-based chat system to communicate.

Teenagers love video games not only because of the social value these games add, but they also provide a challenge and an escape from today's stressors; mental and visual stimuli can help a gamer to forget his or her problems, and for hours on end, forget where they are. As well, they find a sense of value and esteem while playing video games. If you're not a cool or popular kid in school and/or feel powerless in your own daily life, you can become a virtual athlete, a rock star, secret agent, or warrior in a game. Gaming may be the only place that some kids feel totally in control of their lives.[2] As for Jake, I am now aware that gaming has once again become his escape from school.

Interestingly, Atari ™, the brand name of one of the original video game platforms, in Japanese means "you're about to become engulfed". It is appropriately named, as this is what happens for many gamers; they become engulfed in their video game, lose track of time, and stop caring about anything outside of that focus. They lose valuable time that can take away opportunities for these teens to learn other hobbies, activities, and sports. And it can rob them of time to spend on homework and time interacting with their family.[2]

Video games are made to be, in a sense, addictive; game designers are always looking for ways to make their games more interesting and increase the amount of time one will spend playing them. Consequently, games are designed to be just difficult enough to be challenging, but still allowing players to experience small accomplishments, along the way, to compel them to keep playing. And massive, multi-player online role-playing video games can be especially addictive because there is no ending. Teenagers, who are easily bored, have poor relationships with their families, feel like outcasts at school, or tend toward sensation-seeking, may be prone to become addicted to gaming. And those with anxiety, depression, and/or other mental illness issues may be at risk because dopamine levels in players' brains double while they are playing. Dopamine is a mood-regulating hormone that is associated with feelings of pleasure, so it's in essence like taking a drug to make one feel much better. But, in Jake's case, it is ultimately just a temporary fix, and when the gaming continues for lengthy periods of time, affecting one's ability to cope and to even live, the mental illness can take on a more dramatic and dangerous state. Once a gamer has reached high levels of dopamine while playing video games, it can be difficult to find other activities that duplicate this kind of high. This places one at a higher risk of feeling the low and having depressed feelings of withdrawal when they aren't actively gaming. The designers of these games seem to understand this: they build video games that create the high dopamine effect, thus making it harder to put down the console. Video games always have a virtual purpose and a goal to reach, and outside of this activity, finding something that matches the high and also has purpose may be difficult.[3] This seems to be the case for Jake. Although attending school has the goal of getting a degree, studying and learning in class just doesn't match the same sensation he experiences while gaming. It creates self-doubt and stress for him, at times. I can understand Jake's need to want to escape into gaming, and feel this dopamine rush, each time he starts to feel insecure about his ability, and enormous pressure, while trying to make his grades in school.

Clearly, it's important as a parent to monitor the time your teen spends playing video games. I wished I'd recognized much sooner that it was affecting Jake's motivation and his personality. I had chalked it up to so many other things, blindly turning away from a potential issue until it was almost too late. I think this might be the case with many parents. We want to give our child the benefit of the doubt and trust that they are making good choices. I could have taken charge and shut down the gaming units in our home, removing the power cord, his laptop, and his phone. I should have limited his time for playing video games while he was still living under my roof. And once university began, the signs were even clearer; he stopped grooming, he was dirty and so was his dorm room, he was moody and defensive at times, he stopped communicating as often, he was sleeping too much and keeping late hours, and he didn't appear to be doing any schoolwork. Again, I made excuses, not wanting to see that there was a much bigger issue. This would not be one of those times. I now know that Jake is feeling a tremendous amount of pressure again and that the idea of attending classes is terrifying, despite the weeks of counselling, the healthier diet and exercise, and the full support of his family. I cannot ignore the obvious. I must do something more, much more this time.

~~~~~~

Once home, Jake and I have a big discussion in private about how he feels about himself. He explains to me that he feels afraid, and in his fear, he feels physically sick and shaky. He is so full of worry that things will go wrong, that even when things don't fall apart, he just starts fretting over the next event that might. Jake experiences a sense of pressure even when there's none around him. He never feels safe to fail. The fear of failure is now paralyzing him, and waking up each day and accepting it, handling it, and living with it is overwhelming. He's feeling low about himself and perceives his failure to be strong as a weakness.

Whenever I am dealing with clients who are struggling with self-esteem issues, I have a written exercise I use to help them to get more clarity on who they are. There are times in our lives where we can stop taking care of our own needs and see ourselves as unworthy. Sadly, we become self-critical rather than self-loving. Jake has gone there, and he is feeling very low about himself. I don't know what else to do but to try whatever it takes to save him from himself.

In this exercise, I ask the participant to come up with the name of the person they admire the most. This doesn't have to necessarily be someone they know, personally. It can be a famous person, a musician, an actor, a television personality, or it can be a friend or family member, a boss, or co-worker. There are no rules about who to choose. Once the name is established, then I ask them to list all of the reasons that they admire this person, in single words, not in sentences. For example, they might say things like compassionate, funny, fun, tenacious, hardworking, loyal, and honest. Once the list is complete, I then scratch out the name they chose and replace it with their own name. And then I explain that one cannot see the good attributes in another unless they own these same qualities. We are mirrors for each other. But sometimes, in our pain and suffering, and lack of self-esteem, we forget who we are. We work through the exercise together and Jake has a profound moment of self-recognition. His list includes the following: Fun, Funny, Strong, Self-Reliant, Helpful, Insightful, Social/Friendly, Smart, Self-Confident, Wise, Knowing, Attractive, Loving, Loveable, Forgiving. He sees his potential on paper, although in his heart and soul, he doesn't yet believe in it.

Jake confesses that upon entering university he believed that he would do well, academically, and be at the top of the class in his program, which made sense; after all he had come away from secondary school with a diploma showing that he had graduated from the Enrichment Program. He was in the top tier of students at school then. But through first semester he began to see that there were many other gifted students and some of them were scoring higher results in their grades than he was. This shook Jake's confidence and he began to give up on his ability in second semester. He stopped trying. I understood this and how this could happen. I remind Jake that a certificate showing his degree will not show his grades, it will just state that he has attained a degree in his program, and doing his best is what will help him to achieve this. I wanted Jake to stop putting so much pressure on himself to *be* the best, and just *do* the best he can.

"Do you still want to attend university and is this the program that you wish to continue in?" I ask.

He says, with conviction, "Yes and yes."

"Okay then, we will have to come up with a plan that will help you to succeed with that," I say: "I have to ask you again. What do you need? The sky's the limit and if I have to shut my business down temporarily to help you, then I am prepared to do so."

Jake's reply comes as a surprise, but also as relief. He is being honest, and I can only applaud this after months of deception.

"I need you to drive me to university and walk me to classes until I can do it on my own. If you take me back to residence and leave me on my own, I will not attend my courses. I am too scared, and I can't do this alone," he tells me straight.

I realize now just how much his confidence has been shaken, and I see that he feels too paralyzed with fear to move forward. I get it.

"Of course," I tell him. "Okay, that's what we will do, starting on Monday."

I am only happy to do this; I meant it when I said I was willing to do whatever it takes for him to create success. I have no idea what this will look like. I'm making it up as I go along, much like I did when I decided to pull him from Grade One and attempted to homeschool him. But he's told me he needs me, and I am his mother. I will do whatever it takes.

There is homework online for Jake to catch up on for the first week that he has missed, and I am firm that he must spend the weekend completing this. This task will be the first step in Jake taking some responsibility, and hopefully feeling less taxed about catching up on Monday. He has only missed one week of school which can be salvaged pretty quickly.

We talk also about how and why he became so isolated at school and how he turned to the online friendships. He had previously raved about the friendships that he made in year one in his residence and classes, at least until he dropped out of sight into his nightly online gaming sessions. Jake explains to me that in secondary school he knew who his tribe was. He was an accepted member of the group of intellectually-advanced students and had made another smaller group of friends from those in the arts program. He felt a big part of that social network and it was easy to maintain those friendships; they developed with ease and as a result of logistics. And as he muddled through those later teen years and developed more self-awareness, he became more cautious and shy, and began to feel awkward about himself. He accepted that he was part of the intellectual nerd and fine arts groups; they were his tribes and they had been for quite some time, so there was an ease he felt with them. And then, he goes on to explain that he got thrown into a new city, amongst a huge community of university students, and all of them were virtual strangers to him. And then, he had to find and develop a new tribe, but with this new awkwardness within himself. He quickly realized that it could be so much easier to find his new friendships as a faceless player in a virtual world. So, he created a network of friends online, and basically abandoned any idea of making real time friends. And as I listen to him I am aware of something I had previously been naïve about. We watch our children grow up and we see them make friends on the playground with such ease, and we stop paying attention when their ease turns into floundering. We, as adults know the pain of entering a room of strangers and the difficulty of finding our comfort level. Most of us won't start a conversation with a stranger in an elevator, but instead clumsily fidget and watch the buttons on the wall above us. Do we remember when we went from a place of utter abandon to one of caution? I tell Jake that I completely understand his dilemma and am so grateful to him for his candor. I have learned something new and vital, as a parent, and I realize that creating a much-needed social foundation for Jake is not going to be easy, and will take a great deal of effort and time.

Footnotes:

[1] www.pewinternet.org/2015/08/06/chapter-3-video-games-are-key-elements-in-friendships-for-many-boys/

[2] www.oneplace.com/ministries/parenting-teens-weekend/read/articles/teens-obsessed-with-video-games-11951.html

[3] www.gamertherapist.com/2013/08/25/dopey-about-dopamine-video-games-drugs-addiction-2/

An excellent resource for overcoming and stopping video game addiction is: http://gamequitters.com/

Chapter 21

It's a winter's day in Ontario, -10 degrees Celsius and overcast skies. I start thinking about the hour-long drive to Guelph that I will have each day and pray that the weather will co-operate. As I do most weekday mornings, I meet up with my fitness buddy, Cindy, for our five-kilometer power walk. She has been and continues to be a pillar of strength for me during this time. She is someone who is understanding and compassionate, and I have been able to bounce things off her and talk it through. She gives me well-intentioned advice. On this particular morning what she's about to suggest will probably be the biggest lifesaving counsel I could hear. She tells me that getting Jake back on track is not something I should be doing alone, and that I will need much support with this endeavor. She recommends that I leave earlier on my drive today to the university and take Jake straight to the school's Emergency Crisis Center, explain Jake's situation, and ask for a counsellor to be assigned to Jake immediately. That way, he will have someone also at the university essentially in his corner. I instantly feel better hearing this and agree that I will do just as she suggests.

I return home after our walk, feeling more optimistic; I have a viable plan. I don't suggest or ask Jake to consider this. I tell him what we're going to do, and we quickly get ready to leave much earlier, making the first of many trips to come.

The roads are clear of snow and ice and we arrive at the university in good time, park and make the thirteen-minute walk from Jake's residence to the University Center. It's cold and bitterly windy and we make conversation about how far and how chilly the walk is to campus. Jake says that that hasn't helped. Getting out of bed early and making that miserably cold walk wasn't motivating for him in any way. I, myself, am more concerned about the isolated area his residence is in; it always feels like a dead zone when I visit. Inside the main campus building we look for the student crisis office, which is actually called Student Accessibility Services (SAS). My heart starts to race. I am quite nervous about this whole process. This is a delicate situation and I am not sure how we will be received. I am also desperate to have support, as this issue has become much bigger than me. I feel a little panicked already and my heart is racing in my chest. I can only imagine the dread and fear that Jake is experiencing.

We are greeted by a student at reception. She tells us that she is substituting for the secretary, who is on early lunch break. We are told that we will need to come back because there are no counsellors available. I tell her that this situation is an emergency and that we need to speak with someone immediately. She tells me again that we will need to come back later. This setback is not what either of us needs to hear right now, and my panic rises. Jake has classes he needs to get to later, and we have a small window of time to make this happen. The urgency of wanting help rises in my body like a tidal wave. My disappointment quickly sets in and I feel a huge letdown. I feel completely helpless and stranded, similar to what I experienced when we couldn't get a flight out of Huatulco, Mexico. Jake must have also felt this a thousand times over while he spent those two lonely months in his dorm room.

We are about to turn away, defeated, when suddenly a man appears from behind the reception desk. He has overheard our conversation and interjects to ask what it is that we need; his voice and presence carry such kindness, that I am suddenly overwhelmed with emotion. I start to explain Jake's situation and instantly fill up with tears. The man invites us into his office immediately. Our hero has arrived, and I now feel intense relief and hopefulness. It is almost dizzying. I need to sit.

The man introduces himself and his position. He tells us that he personally will not be taking on Jake's case, but can initiate it and get him into the system where counselling will be assigned. But first he needs the particulars. Jake begins his story and articulates in great detail his challenges, both past and present.

The counsellor is first astounded by the fact that Jake was placed in the "Family Units" for residence, a place of isolation and quiet, where mostly student couples reside and remain to themselves. He explains that there are rarely any social activities initiated there, and it would not be a good placement for Jake. He suggests that we get Jake transferred to a dorm room back on campus, as soon as possible. We agree wholeheartedly. He understands this, and I begin to relax.

The counsellor suggests that Jake is suffering with some sort of anxiety disorder, and he proposes that I take him to our family doctor and have him fully assessed immediately. There are required documents that will need to be filled out and signed by the doctor, and then returned to the university SAS office before anything more can be put in motion. He then explains to us that once this was in place, Jake would be assigned a Special Needs Advisor, who would discuss any modifications needed to his program. He would also be assigned a counsellor who he would visit with regularly to help him to sort out and manage his anxiety while attending school.

To save time and get Jake the help he needs as soon as possible, we make an appointment with the Special Needs Advisor as well as one with the residence head. We both gratefully thank this kind man, and then leave the office with a sense of accomplishment, feeling heard and understood. Cindy was right; this is exactly what is needed to give both

Jake and I a sense that we are not going to have to handle this alone. We make our way to the next campus building where Jake will begin his very first second semester class. This will be my next test in surrender and trust.

~~~~~~

We enter the school building and find the room where Jake's English class will take place. There is already a group of students forming outside of the lecture hall. I realize that I need to use a bathroom and decide to leave Jake in the hall to wait until the class ahead lets out so that he can go in and find a seat. I disappear down another hall and use the facility. When I return, the students are gone, and the lecture hall door is closed. I assume, at first, that Jake has entered the class, but then I am suddenly hit with panic. Due to the nature of Jake's fragile state, and my being very aware of his fear response, I become concerned that Jake may very well be at risk to run away rather than face his first lecture. I have no idea if he fled from the school when I turned a corner or if he did, in fact go into the classroom. I feel like a failure; I question, once again whether I did step in and support him or whether I let him down by walking away and leaving him on his own. I console myself with the thought that I might likely have embarrassed him to have stood in the hall by his side, while the other students were waiting for class to start. He did, after all, say that he needed me to walk him to class, not shadow him every second of his school day. I feel caught in limbo, between that invisible line of knowing when to step in and when to back off. I can now only sit and wait and hope that Jake did the right thing.

While waiting, I run into the son of a friend of mine who is also attending this university and who is in second year. It's delightful to see a familiar face, especially when I am feeling so frazzled. He provides a momentary bit of calm and distraction. He sits down with me in the lobby and we have a chat and catch up. I explain to him that Jake is returning after a difficult first semester, and that I am there for moral support. This fine young man, very kind and sweet, helps to keep me company while I try to calm my nerves. The conversation certainly helps to pass the time until he has to leave for his next lecture.

Soon Jake's lecture door opens, and the students begin streaming out into the hall. I watch with bated breath for Jake's appearance. The hall quickly empties and there's no sign of Jake. My heartbeat quickens and my greatest fear that I messed up creates panic in me. A few minutes pass and still no Jake. I am fully panicked and start asking myself just where Jake took off to. How am I going to find him? How am I going to help him work out this dilemma? My mind starts racing. I feel truly hopeless. This plan is not going well, and I am running out of ideas as to how to make it work. I tell myself that maybe it's a mistake to have him return to school this semester; that he may not be ready for this at all. I pick up my phone and I text Jake to ask where he is. He doesn't answer. More time passes. I am freaking out inside.

And then I see him coming out of the lecture hall. The relief hits me like a rock, and I want to cry with abandon. But I don't. I won't let Jake see that I momentarily lost trust in him.

"Sorry mom, I couldn't answer your text because I was speaking with my professor about the class, and I was getting more clarity on whether or not I should remain in both English classes," Jake tells me.

"And what is the verdict?" I ask.

"It turns out that there is a lot of crossover. The courses are similar; and it makes sense for me to take only one of them," he says.

I feel so much better hearing this news. Not only did Jake walk in, sit down, and engage in the English course lecture, but he also took the initiative to have a conversation with the professor to make a decision about how best to move forward. Jake has just shown me that he wants to be here, that he wants to attend classes, and he wants to do what is best for him. It's a far better scenario than the one that I had just played out in my head. It's a great start! I feel so proud and happy for Jake. Next step is for him to speak with the head of his computer science program and see what he can replace that second English course with.

With each class that Jake attends on that first day the more settled and less afraid he begins to feel. And the more relaxed I am. English class has now been changed to a computer design course, which will be far more enjoyable and easier for Jake since this is where he really excels. Jake is very creative and loves to sketch and paint. This class will allow him to share his creativity and hear feedback on his progress. This course will be another good area for building his confidence.

At the end of the day we take that long, brisk walk back to my vehicle to drive home. Jake doesn't want to go into his residence room at all now; it is a reminder of a very painful time for him, and he wants to avoid re-living that feeling. So, we just hop straight into my Jeep. We both feel an enormous sense of relief about the day, and I congratulate Jake for having the courage to get through it all. It's going to be important to acknowledge each of the victories as they come, both small and large.

Chapter 22

It's day two of new beginnings for Jake and I, and we start the morning first by seeing our family physician. We explain to him that although Jake had some success with the eight weeks of counselling, returning to school on his own again was just too much to manage, and that he took a step backwards in his progress. We also outlined the process that took place the day before at school with SAS and that Jake now requires a medical assessment and the necessary paperwork to be filled out. With this in place Jake would be able to receive the services he needs from the school's counselling department.

Upon hearing all of this, our GP immediately asks, "Are we now ready to accept my earlier diagnosis of Attention Deficit Disorder?"

Jake and I had discussed this ahead of time and both agreed that ADD was definitely something to now consider. The walls of denial must be taken down and I am now accepting that Jake's issues in school may have always stemmed from this possibility. Jake admits that his organizational skills are lacking, he's easily distracted, and has difficulty staying focused on mundane tasks. He always blamed his frustrations on school but is now ready to consider that he has some responsibility in how he behaves, as well. I concur.

We unanimously reply, "Yes."

As a holistic health practitioner, I believe that the services I offer are a complement to conventional medicine. I do not describe myself as someone who offers an alternative option to getting one's health back on track. I am fascinated by science and the advancements it's made and continues to make in terms of providing us healthier, longer lives. There is still a great need for surgeons, obstetricians, oncologists, scientists, doctors, and nurses who work hard in medical centers, research facilities, and hospitals. I am not pro natural remedies and against pharmaceutical medicines. There is a need and there is room for both of these. And when I have felt strongly that medical intervention and the use of prescription medicine is the best answer, then, of course I have supported and used these, both with myself and my sons. I believe it's also a personal choice, and education is important in making these decisions. It's vital to consider the side effects, the duration of time they take to become effective, and the state of one's physical constitution before making a sound choice. I also believe that when one makes the decision to use a pharmaceutical drug to treat a condition, it's also vitally important that the person supports his or her system with a healthy diet and a moderate amount of exercise. And in terms of treating a mental health issue, I think it's also equally important to add therapeutic support, either with group or individual counselling from a psychologist, psychiatrist, or a social worker. In my work, I have witnessed those who are in what appear to be mild, moderate, or acute states of anxiety and/or depression. They come to me with the diagnosis, from a doctor, many asking if there is a natural method which they can use to cope with their mental state. All of them have been offered a medication for treatment, but some are not sure if they want to proceed, while others have taken pharmaceuticals in the past, and are looking for a different method to reduce their malaise. Ethically-speaking, I am not in a position in my work to advise a client whether or not they should take what a doctor has prescribed to them, and I am clear with them about this. I also believe that when one is in a state of severe emotional crisis, one where daily functioning is paralyzed or inadequate, that the prescribed medication is the wisest option for stabilizing them in the moment. A healthy diet, exercise, and a good counsellor should still be considered, to make the client feel they have some control over their condition. This approach may perhaps aid them in eventually managing their mental health, without the use of a pharmaceutical drug. I can provide the information only, and the choice ultimately is with the individual. There is room for both conventional and holistic or natural medicines, and value in both. When handled responsibly, both of these options can be of great benefit to those who are unwell and looking to make a choice that feels the best fit for them.

The doctor gives Jake a questionnaire for assessing ADD to fill out, but he already knows what the outcome of this will be. He then discusses with Jake and I some of the issues he was observing that led him to this determination. He also suggests, once again, that Jake consider taking medication for ADD. Jake had told me earlier in the day that he definitely didn't want to be medicated. I fully supported this decision, not only because Jake is an adult and should be able to make that call, but because Jake has always demonstrated difficulty in processing pharmaceutical medications without developing uncomfortable side effects. ADD medications work well over the short term about 70% of the time, and as to the long-term effects, there isn't much research. There also isn't enough information to show the long-term effects that medication has on the brain. But the potential side effects of medication used to treat ADD are well known; these are risk of hallucinations, tics, low-grade depression, and weight loss.[4] Given the fact that Jake had recently lost so much weight, it was clear that neither of us wanted to risk having him lose his appetite and fall back off the weight curve once again. I truly believed medicating him would not be a good fit. For others it may be just what is needed, but I knew instinctively that this wouldn't be the case for him. Jake does, however, agree that we can try using naturopathic remedies and continue with healthy eating and exercise, and so we tell the doctor that this is our choice.

The doctor suggests that he give us two weeks to try this and that we should then check in and re-visit the option of drugs if the alternative remedies aren't effective. He also says that he believes that Jake is suffering from severe depression and anxiety, and that he wishes to include this diagnosis on the SAS forms to ensure that Jake receive the kind of support he feels he needs from the school. We are both so desperate to have Jake surrounded by care and not feel so alone while at school, that we agree with the diagnosis, and are grateful when leaving the office that the paperwork is ready to return to the school immediately. It's another victory and a huge sense of relief for both of us.

I drive to the university with a renewed sense of optimism. Thankfully, although it's winter and a frigid -18 degrees Celsius, the sky is a brilliant blue, the sun is shining brightly, and the roads are clear for driving. Although it would seem that driving for two hours a day during the winter would be a lot for me to shoulder, having that one-on-one time to talk with Jake is critical. For Jake, he gets an opportunity to talk to me about all of the stressors he had faced alone last semester, with no one to discuss them with, and now he is able to get a lot off of his chest. As well, Jake can share with me what some of his fears are now, in second semester. For me, I get a clearer picture of what Jake was going through then and how he is feeling now and can offer him some comfort and parental advice as he moves forward. This exchange is something he shut me out of in first semester, and I now hope that he sees its significance as he progresses. We mothers can't help it. We anticipate being needed for support and advice, as we are natural nurturers. That doesn't end when our children become adults.

At school Jake takes the completed Special Needs Assessment forms to the SAS office, and is then able to book an appointment with a counsellor for the following day. He attends another class and then sorts out his Ontario Student Assistance Program (OSAP) file to show that he is now a registered student once again and will no longer be required to start making payments. I can now have his Registered

Education Savings Fund deferred until next year and will not lose any of the funds we saved. He re-instates his school meal plan and flex card so that he can purchase school supplies and food. And then we leave for home celebrating more small victories and talk about what transpired in Jake's classes.

The following day we are up early and heading back to Guelph, and we discuss today's strategy during the drive. For the past two days I have walked Jake to his classrooms and then waited outside nearby in a lobby or alcove until he is finished. I have spent this time either reading chapters in a novel and/or answering emails and texting. I also want to include my husband in this journey and keep him abreast of Jake's day, especially as he is away on a business trip at this time. Today I need to see a client that I could not re-schedule, so Jake agrees to try going to classes and appointments on his own. I know that it is going to create some anxiety for both of us. I want Jake to feel trusted and capable, and tell myself that if it doesn't work out, then we've only lost a day, and we can return to plan A. Before class begins I drop Jake off at the school for his counselling appointment and then I return home to work in my office. This means four hours total driving time but an opportunity for both of us to get some things accomplished.

Jake keeps me posted via text as he navigates his way, solo. I return to pick him up at the end of the day and congratulate him on getting through it on his own. He shares with me his happiness with the new counsellor he's been assigned and talks about some of what transpired during their session together. I sense immediately that this is going to be a really good fit for Jake. A university counsellor has good insight and understanding into the kinds of issues a special needs student would be struggling with, and how to manage them more effectively. These counselling sessions will be a great addition to the eight weeks of counselling he had previous to this. The day has been fruitful, and so worth the four hours of driving. When we get home, we are greeted by Brian, who has returned from his business trip, and we have an intimate family dinner together. It's early in this new school journey, but I already feel more hopeful, and far less alone. I hope that Jake does, too.

Jake is building a positive momentum and has gained more confidence. Today, while I sit reading in a comfy sofa at the university coffee shop, Jake attends two classes. I have now begun to read a book written by a Canadian psychologist, Gabor Maté, called *Scattered Minds: the Origins and Healing of Attention Deficit Disorder*. I am hungry to learn and understand this disorder, in order to help Jake. I'm drawn to this particular book after reading the following statement online in a Chapters Books review: "Written from the inside by a person who himself has ADD, with the wisdom gained through years of medical practice and research, *Scattered Minds* explodes the myth of ADD as a genetically based illness, offering real hope and advice for children and adults who live with this disorder." I am searching for something that will speak to me, as a holistic practitioner, and have read some of Maté's other works, and his theories resonate with my professional and personal truth. I also wish to have a better understanding of ADD, so that I can be the most help for Jake. So far, this is an excellent read, and I am absorbing it like a sponge. Information can't come to me fast enough, and I am on a quest to be as educated as possible in order to better understand and sustain Jake, in his needs.

And again, from the book:

"Never at rest the mind of the ADD adult flits about like some deranged bird that can light here or there for a while but is perched nowhere long enough to make a home. Attention Deficit Disorder is defined by three major features, any two of which suffice for the diagnosis; poor attention skills, deficient impulse control, and hyperactivity. The hallmark of ADD is an automatic, unwilled "tuning out", a frustrating non-presence of mind. People suddenly find that they have heard nothing of what they were listening to, saw nothing of what they were looking at, and remember nothing of what they were trying to concentrate on. One misses information and directions, misplaces things, and struggles to stay abreast of conversations. The distractibility fosters chaos. Completely lacking in the ADD mind is a template for order, a mental model of how order comes about. The distractibility in ADD is not consistent. A facility for focusing when one is interested in something does not rule out ADD, but to be able to focus the person with ADD needs a much higher level of motivation than do other people."[5]

Reading this it is easy for me to recognize some of these signs in Jake, in varying degrees. I cannot deny that he definitely needs support in finding and maintaining some sort of calm and order to his day-to-day living. And I see evidence of how much counselling, a healthy diet, and exercise has been helping Jake to maintain more focus. We will see how much better he manages once we add a supplement or two to his regimen.

When Jake is let out of his second class we have lunch together in his favourite school cafeteria. I'm impressed that Jake is willing to hang out with his mom while on campus and appears not to care what anyone else thinks. And quite frankly, I don't see anyone making a fuss. For all they know, I could be a mature student he is having lunch with. I make a mental note that I should bring a school type bag and try to blend in a little more, for his sake. During our lunch Jake shares with me how happy he is with the computer courses that he is taking. He describes in great detail what they are studying. Some of this is like listening to a foreign language for me, but I don't have to understand every word of it to know that it is making Jake feel excited and happy. So, I listen and smile, nodding as appropriate.

Following our lunch break, Jake attends his lab, and then we meet up for an interview with the head of residence. We learn that Jake has been approved for a move from his present room to South residence, which is on campus and gives him easier accessibility to classes. It's also busier and has more social interaction so that Jake will feel less isolated. We're both extremely happy with this news; this provides Jake a fresh start and removes him from a space that has felt quite negative and has only served to remind him how dark and desperate he felt while living there.

We return to Caledon, and then attend a fitness class together, working harder than we've ever worked before. At home we express how good it felt to exercise so vigorously. Jake has found much value in fitness and says it helps to make him feel better inside and out. I can definitely see the difference it has made. Jake is now grooming more frequently and taking pride in his physique. He has gained back much of the weight that he had lost during first semester, and he has built some new muscle mass. He looks stronger and he says he feels stronger. It has certainly helped that the fitness instructor, Sue, is not hard core; she's sweet and gentle, and has a compassionate soul. Sue has been concerned about Jake's condition, as well, and goes out of her way to make Jake feel welcome in this fitness class full of middle-aged women. She shows him kindness and encouragement both in and out of class. She even sends him special email messages as his fitness level improves. We have been blessed with amazing support during this journey and are truly grateful.

Day five and the end of it marks one full week since Jake has begun to attend classes, seminars, and labs. His confidence has begun to rise, and he feels happy to be a part of something again. He has purpose, he has goals, and he is meeting these. It's still one day at a time, and we are completely aware that we're still white-knuckling through this. The appointment for Jake to meet with his assigned Special Needs Advisor is not scheduled until the end of the month, which is making Jake a little anxious. Thankfully, he has another meeting scheduled with his counsellor for next week. Jake is starting to see how having these regular consultations is providing him with accountability and having someone to check in with helps to keep him on track. The herbal remedy order that I placed earlier in the week has arrived, and in it are supplements that Jake can now start taking to support his body and help with the ADD. He begins to take them that evening, and in order to remember to ingest these capsules twice a day, I suggest that he sets a special alarm on his cell phone. I recognize that I will need to monitor closely how well the combination of healthy diet, exercise, the supplement, and the counselling sessions are helping Jake to manage his ADD and anxiety.

Footnotes:

[4] http://www.psychiatryadvisor.com/adhd/why-treat-adhd-without-medication/article/416841/

[5] Scattered Minds: How Attention Deficit Disorder Originates and What you Can Do About It by Gabor Mate, M.D., Plume Publishing/2000, Chapter 1 - So Much Soup and Garbage Can, page 4

Chapter 23

It's the second week of my new Saturday morning Circuit Training with Cindy, and Jake is also getting up and joining us. He seems to be thriving with exercise and enjoys the classes. Nick has come home for a visit. It's always a highlight for me when all of my family is together in one room. It's always great for Jake, too. He and Nick have such an amazing bond. It's a joy to watch them in action. They get together and talk and laugh non-stop. We have a fabulous family dinner, one of our favourites, lamb. And then we drive together to a theatre that is not too far out of town and see a stand-up comedy show; lots of laughs, much needed, and a good way to cap off Jake's first triumphant week at school.

In mid-January we make the very painful decision to return our recently-adopted dogs, Duff and Roo, back to the pound. I realize that with all of the travelling back and forth to Guelph, and the dogs' anxiety with separation, I just can't provide them with the kind of attention they require. Their behaviour has become far too disruptive for our lives, as well. Each day that I return from Guelph I find a mess in the kitchen that requires a half hour of cleaning up and two distressed animals hungry for an insatiable amount of attention. Although they give us all so much love and affection and serve as a much-needed temporary distraction to the challenges we've had to face in our personal lives, they are also very high maintenance. I am becoming resentful of cleaning up after them after a long day and a lengthy drive home, and it is not fair to the dogs. I need to focus all of my energies on Jake's needs right now. So it's heartbreaking to know I have to return them to the shelter, and it will seem empty in the house without them. But I am at peace and know that I am making the right decision, even though saying good-bye to these beautiful boys is tremendously painful for our family.

On Monday morning I help Jake move from his old townhouse school residence to the new one he's been assigned to. This one is on campus and is in a much busier and more socially active area. He had hoped to be in a room, sharing with other students, but he is in a pod, and each of the students has a separate room. There's no common sitting room, just a hallway and a shared bathroom. It seems a tad impersonal, but we focus on the fact that it's a closer walk to campus. The hope is that Jake will eventually feel he is able to start sleeping in residence rather than coming home every day. He attends class and then a lab and then we are on our way home.

I host Book Club that evening, and Jake has homework to complete. I later learn that he had allowed himself to become distracted by watching television, and now he has to make up for lost time sometime tomorrow. I don't want to come down on Jake about this; he does need downtime, but he also needs to recognize when enough is enough and set his priorities in terms of his schoolwork. I can see how he became easily distracted and then turned to online video gaming. I think we can all get into those kinds of funks, where we want to bail on life, sit and do something completely mindless. And after some of the reading on ADD, I see that this is a very real challenge for Jake. We will need to work together to find some strategies to help him stay focused. Jake takes full responsibility for his actions, and is now determined to do whatever it takes to catch up on his school assignments.

It's the third week of January and Jake and I are both in a happier place. Although I spent four hours today driving back and forth between the university and home, I was able to drop Jake off to fend for himself, while I took some much needed Me-time. Jake successfully managed the day, on his own, and got a lot of schoolwork accomplished. His first English assignment is now complete, and he tells me that he was able to meet up with the students with whom he's doing a group project in computer class. Meanwhile, I was able to have lunch with a friend. I so appreciated this opportunity for some time to just relax and enjoy a meal and conversation with another woman. Jake is working hard and proving that he really wants to succeed in this semester, which allows me to relax and enjoy a little down time.

Each day that we drive to Guelph we both comment on the colourful ice fishing huts that we see cropping up on Guelph Lake. And each time I say that I'd love to photograph them. So, on Tuesday morning I drop Jake off at university and then drive down the road to the lake. It is a gorgeous, sunny day, although very cold, and I want to capture a few images of some of the ice fishing activity. I packed my photography gear and had purposely dressed more warmly and have my winter mukluks on, so navigating down the wooded area and onto the ice should be easy. Part way down the woods I meet an ice fisher named Andre who has already scoped out the area he wants to set up on. He has his sled full of equipment and is heading to the ice surface. I ask him if he'd mind if I take some pictures and he is quite gracious about allowing me to do so. The whole idea of someone spending a day on an extremely cold surface just to catch a few fish is absolutely fascinating to me, so I ask Andre many questions as I follow along and watch him prepare for his day. First, to settle my nervousness about walking across the ice, he tells me that it is thick enough to drive a truck over.

Cautiously walking across the ice, and focused upon staying steady on my feet, I ask Andre just what kind are caught in this particular lake. He tells me he can catch Pickerel, Pike, and

Crappies. I am also wondering how one knows when it is a good day to fish, as Jake and I had noticed that some days the area is much busier with fishing huts than others. I learn that when the winds are coming from the west, then fishing will be good, but when it comes from the east, the fishermen stay home. Andre tells me that fish are most active early in the morning, and then again in early afternoon. And the colder the day, the better, as frigid waters make for the firmest and flakiest fish, which equals better eating.

The equipment that Andre brought is quite extensive, and I can see that anyone who ice fishes must take their safety very seriously. Andre has spikes to add to his boots to grip the ice better, something I am wishing I had thought of, as I continue to fear losing my balance on this very slippery surface. He has a propane powered auger to help drill the hole in the ice, and a slotted metal ladle to screen out the floating ice bits after drilling so that they won't freeze up on his fishing line. He also has a propane heater to keep his fishing hut warm throughout the day. It is all very fascinating to me, and after an hour of taking photographs of Andre and a few others who have set up to fish, I leave feeling like I've got more than a few good pictures. I've gained a better understanding and a whole new respect for those who love to ice fish. I don't walk away with any fish, but I am satisfied in getting the shots I wanted, and it was a great way to decompress, relax, and not have to think or worry about Jake. It's a welcome reprieve.

In the meantime, I learn that Jake is having a morning of challenges, and has sent me a text telling me about his mishaps. I was so preoccupied with my morning ice mission that I left my cell phone in my vehicle. And as it turns out, he sorted through it all on his own, handling it all with grace and humour. I really hadn't had anything to worry about after all. I return home to load the photographs onto my computer, excited to see how they would turn out, and then proceed to photo edit and then share them online.

Besides my small photography expedition, the highlight of my day is then receiving a later text from Jake exclaiming that he has made a new friend at school. He starts talking with a fellow student on the way out of English class, and then they decide to have coffee together and chat some more. He is so happy to have made a connection, and I am elated that things are starting to fall into place and Jake is beginning to have a more typical university experience. Another small victory to celebrate! I get a bit of a driving break, as Jake's dad offers to drive him home from school this evening. They will be going out for dinner together while I attend a business network event. I enjoy these events as I get to see some familiar faces, and also meet some new business women. And I have the opportunity to learn new business strategies from the guest speakers. Any bit of normalcy in my life is a welcome change, and for the evening I am able to focus on myself and my business and forget about the challenge of getting Jake through this semester.

Chapter 24

    Today Jake decides that he wants to try staying overnight in residence. I am very nervous about the concept, and so is he, but we agree to give it a try. I drop Jake off at school and we agree to stay in touch by text throughout the day and evening as part of our support plan. I then drive up the road to visit with my friend, Iris, who has moved to Guelph just a few months ago. I met Iris back in 1985 when I lived and worked in Mississauga. Her daughter, Barbara, had been shot and left a quadriplegic as the result of a convenience store robbery, and she was looking for a full time attendant. I was hired and worked with her for the following eighteen months. It was a job I loved, and if it were not for the unfortunate car accident I was involved in, I would have continued working with Barb for much longer. While I was in the home and helping Barb with her daily routine, I also helped to tidy up and prepare meals for the family, as Iris was a single working mom of five daughters, four of whom still lived at home; I felt it would relieve her stresses to have a hot meal for her and her girls to come home to as often as possible. There were also times that Barb required my assistance for an evening event she was attending, and so I became a larger part of her family life and got to know her, her sisters and her mom quite well. To this day, we all still keep in touch. And Iris, the matriarch, is someone whom I have a deep respect for and I enjoy her company immensely.

I had called Iris the day before to tell her I would be coming to Guelph. She invites me to come to her new home for breakfast. It was exactly what I needed, so I accept. All of the driving back and forth, all of the stress of getting Jake through the last few months, it's all wearing pretty thin on me, and to be treated to a warm breakfast and welcoming company is so nice. Iris doesn't know just what has transpired with Jake, and so I begin to share the story with her while we eat. I break down in tears at times, and as the tale unfolds I begin to realize the heavy toll all of this is having on me. I am also discovering that the more I share, the more supported I feel. Honestly, I don't know what I'd do without the comfort of my female friends. I have always believed that my girlfriends save my life every day, and I am now truly testing them with this. I leave after breakfast feeling more positive and assured that Jake is going to manage fine with his overnight stay in residence.

Jake and I stay in touch throughout the day and evening by text and then on the phone. He tells me that he has finally met his residence mates, that he's attended all of his classes today and worked on school assignments. At 11:00 p.m. we say good night, and I work really hard to let go, stay calm and get a good night's sleep. Nothing about my night is easy, and restful sleep is impossible.

~~~~~~

It's day ten of me driving Jake to school and the first day that he is being picked up from school after spending a night in residence. Jake has been taking his remedies for ADD diligently and says that they seem to be helping. He is managing to do well and is attending all classes. But I worry that if there are not more supports in place with the school then I will have many more weeks of driving Jake and having him sleep at home each night. Although Jake reported to me, via text that he had a good day and was on task, when I pick him up from school at the end of today I can instantly see that he'd had some struggles and had not been truthful with me. I have now learned the cues that tell me when Jake is lying, and

I also trust my sixth sense, intuition, or maternal radar, whatever one wants to call it. Jake's eyes dilate more, his body gets shaky, and he has difficulty making eye contact. His talk is far more upbeat, almost like he's putting on a show of being perfectly capable and in a really good place. So, I tell him immediately that it's okay if things didn't go as planned. I want Jake to feel just as comfortable talking about the challenges as he does when talking about successes. I also don't want to waste any time talking in circles while he tries to hide the truth and deny an opportunity for growth. It's vitally important that he owns his truth and takes responsibility for his actions.

He eventually confesses to me, "Mom, I lost all focus last night and I didn't actually get my school assignments completed. I wasted time on my computer binge watching YouTube videos instead."

I am not surprised. I knew this would be tough for Jake to handle so soon.

I tell him, "It's okay. It was great that you attempted an overnight, on your own. Perhaps you're not ready for that step just yet. We are not striving for perfection, and we should appreciate any attempt to move forward," I say.

I know that he still has many fears, that he is still struggling with the online video withdrawal, his anxiety and ADD, and that much of this process will require a great deal of discipline and maturity. I think about how I behaved at his age and recall how ill-equipped I was at handling many adult issues. This struggle will take more time and patience from both of us. In the meantime, Jake has more school work to catch up on, and the responsibility still lies on his shoulders to get it done.

~~~~~~

It's Saturday and time for circuit training again. It's great that Jake is still participating. During the week he often joins Cindy and I for the very early 6:00 a.m. classes, and says it's really helping him feel good about his body and his emotions. I strongly believe that exercise can strengthen one's physical and mental health, and provide an outlet for stress, so I'm happy to see that Jake is gaining something so positive for his efforts.

Much of my time has been spent on seeing Jake through the past two weeks of school, and so following fitness class I decide to take a drive into the city and visit with Nick. Our relationship has regained its closeness and I now look forward to our visits. He is a great city guide, always happy to show me around his neighbourhood. We snoop through the shops and I treat Nick to a haircut at a salon not far from his place, owned and also operated by our friend, Erica. We get to visit with her while Nick gets a new look. We have a great afternoon, and I bring Nick up to speed on how Jake is doing with school. He's surprised that I've had to drive Jake to classes each day to settle him into university. He also recognizes that Jake is still vulnerable to a setback and asks me what he can do to help. I realize that in many families, an older brother in this position might be curious, and may even be concerned about the situation, but might not offer to help. Nick is not that kind of person, that kind of son, or that kind of brother. He has always come from a heartfelt, good place, and has always had an instinct for doing what is right and what is noble. And although I didn't expect this, I am not surprised. It is a welcome gesture. Adding another helper into the mix would ultimately help both Jake and I. It doesn't take me long to think of a way to have Nick involved in this process, and I start explaining that the next step would be to fully integrate Jake back into residence life, which means remaining at the campus and sleeping in his residence each weeknight. Jake is definitely not ready to take this step on his own just yet, and in fact may never be able to, this semester, but it's worth an attempt to see if he can manage it. Without hesitation, Nick suggests that he can conduct his work responsibilities, virtually, from the university campus, and offers to take a week of his time and move into Jake's dorm room and help him to navigate his way into his new residence. It's a great idea, and one I know that Jake will be on board with. We agree to give Jake one more week of classes while I continue to drive, and then Nick can join him at school. I leave Nick and the city feeling more hopeful and so relieved to have another person on board to rally around Jake. It truly does take a village to raise even an adult child.

I have begun recording and watching a weekly television program called Super Soul Sunday, on the recommendation of a friend. It has become a bit of a church service for me, and spiritual food for thought. Well-known icon, Oprah Winfrey, created this series and I had heard only good things about it, so I decided there would be no greater time than now to take a little break once a week and view it. One of the shows has really resonated for me with regard to the situation Jake is in. There was something about the message that I believed would be important for him to hear, so I told him I'd watched it and would be willing to watch it again if he would like to see it with me. I really didn't know what to expect. Jake could be very resistant to this sort of thing, but he surprised me and agreed to see it.

Oprah was interviewing Timothy Shriver and they were discussing a book that he had written called *Fully Alive*. Mr. Shriver was explaining that the book was drawn from his own personal experience, his growing up among the famous Kennedy families. His mother was sister to assassinated U.S. President, John F. Kennedy, and the family had suffered many such tragedies throughout the years. Mr. Shriver went on to say that no one in his family ever spoke of these significant family losses, and in fact were encouraged to use their energies for more important duties. As someone from privilege, they had an obligation to those less fortunate, and they had work to do. In essence, he was taught the message that there was no time for grieving; one raised in privilege was taught he or she had an important job to do in serving others. And then later in life, he experienced a situation that made him realize that by never grieving, never talking about death, and never having counsel for his emotions, he never felt fully alive. It was only in finally allowing himself to feel and work through the grief that he believed he was able to finally start living. Much of the interview between Ms. Winfrey and Mr. Shriver is very touching and emotional for me. I look over at Jake and see that he too is wiping away tears. I don't say anything but have a sense and a hope that watching this is creating an internal shift for him.

On the way to school, later that morning Jake starts to talk with me about his personal perspective after watching that Super Soul Sunday episode. He truly did have an aha moment during the interview. Jake shared that when he heard Mr. Shriver speak about the emptiness he felt for not grieving, it struck a chord in him. He realized in the moment that he heard those words, that he himself had never allowed himself to grieve for the loss of his grandfather, or the loss of his beloved dog, Thunder, or for the sadness he experienced feeling ostracized and overwhelmed during middle school, or for any other times that he felt sad but had pushed it down and refused to look at it. And in hearing someone else say that he felt fully alive after finally grieving, Jake came to the realization that it was okay to feel sad, and that he needs to still allow that to come through him in some way. He then explained to me that he felt less anxious and more at peace for knowing this, and that he was prepared to start acknowledging and feeling his own personal sadness.

I didn't know whether to be more grateful for the television program, Oprah, Timothy Shriver, or Jake's ability to have that kind of insight and honesty with himself. It was all such a remarkable gift. I so appreciated the fact that Jake was able to share this with me. It is not always easy to express such vulnerability, and after all that Jake has been through these last several months, this self-discovery is an incredible breakthrough for him. Jake is another step closer to healing and creating a new place from which to launch forward, one with depth and honesty, and self-awareness. He is only nineteen years old, but he seems to be now operating from a place of great maturity, wisdom, and authenticity. I am in awe, and I wonder who is teaching whom now. Our children and their perspective and awareness is like an unwrapped present, and if we never take moments like this to listen and truly understand who they are, that package remains sealed, and we lose an opportunity to really know and learn from them. This moment is special, and I certainly do not take it for granted. I don't know what Jake's plan is for him to fully experience his tender years of loss and sadness, and I am not sure he does, at this moment, either. But I applaud him for his integrity and willingness to grow and am witnessing a young man who is hungry to do and feel better. I can't ask any more of him in this moment. I do offer to add an herbal remedy to his vitamin regime, one that will support his nervous system through his grieving. I now see that he has probably felt depressed for quite some time and hasn't been able to shake it on his own. His body needs support. Jake agrees that this may help, and the following day starts taking a Chinese remedy I am familiar with that will work to bring more balance in his system and help him to cope a little easier through the next part of his journey.

Chapter 25

It will be a couple more weeks before Nick can live in residence with Jake. He needs time to organize this with work, and then Jake will be coming home to break for Reading Week. In the meantime, Brian and I take turns with driving duties to the university and back. This small break allows me some much-needed time to focus on myself and my business. Brian has such a busy work schedule that I appreciate any time that he can spare. I take time to rest, and I also see clients and attend a couple of business network meetings. It is good to be around my business associates; these are relationships I have nurtured and have received a tremendous amount of support from, not just in terms of business but also in my personal life.

The winter weather this month has been brutally cold with high wind chill factors, but for the most part we have received little snowfall, and the roads have been clear for driving. Later in the week, we get a snowfall that prevents us one evening from retrieving Jake from school, and he successfully spends a night on his own in residence. He is starting to turn a corner.

Jake returns home with me on the Friday evening; he feels happy that he had a successful first meeting with his Special Needs Advisor. Together they have arranged for some modifications to Jake's program. In order to reduce his anxiety, he will be given extra time and a separate room to take his tests and exams in, as needed. She has also suggested that a Peer Support Student may be helpful in offering Jake more accountability and leverage; someone who can check in on him and offer an extra foothold as Jake works through school assignments and obligations. This will be a third or fourth year student volunteer, and so he will have to wait to see who will be available for this role. It is one more piece that we are both grateful will be eventually added to the package that will aid Jake in achieving a more successful semester. Jake also feels happy that the week has worked out well. Classes have been interesting, and he met with his new friend again, managed an overnight in residence, is working hard and seems to be in a good place. He feels the added naturopathic remedy is also helping to take the edge off so that he can deal with his sadness; he feels more upbeat and calmer. Week three of semester two is behind us, with more work to do, but it somehow feels a much lighter load as we celebrate more small victories that are adding up to a brighter future for Jake.

We spend the weekend together as a family. Jake gets in some time on the slopes snowboarding on Saturday before we drive to Nick's apartment to give him a hand with moving some furniture. We all spend Sunday together in our family home with Jake doing school assignments, and Nick giving him some much appreciated guidance with his English project. The guys play table tennis, and then we all make dinner together - braised beef ribs and caramelized onions, another favourite. We sit down to watch the annual Super Bowl football match on the television, but I make it only halfway through before succumbing to complete exhaustion, and then find my way to bed.

Chapter 26

It's now February and our plans for returning Jake to residence with Nick are delayed due to a huge winter storm that brought 20 centimeters of snow. All schools are closed, including universities. For the entire time that Nick attended, I don't ever remember the university closing classes. The consequence is that we have another day of togetherness at home, something I always love. Honestly, I think that this kind of closeness with my family is what fuels my spirit the most; it keeps me grounded and makes everything in the world feel right. Thankfully, the snowstorm didn't create any power outages in the area, so I am able to get into my kitchen to make two hearty winter soups and start a lovely dinner in the slow cooker. Board games are brought out to play, and Nick and Jake also take some time for playing table tennis. I enjoy hearing the Ping-Pong ball bouncing back and forth below me on the table in the basement, as well as their laughter. I am reminded once again how blessed I am to have raised two sons who not only respect and love each other, but also really like each other's company. My own childhood home with my three brothers was often filled with irritation and verbal and physical fighting. After dinner the weather is calm, and Brian and I decide that it is clear enough to drive the guys to the university. Jake has early morning classes the next day, so they can start their routine in the morning, already in residence.

Four days at home, free of my responsibilities with Jake, feels like a mini vacation. Not that I am ready to shirk my duties as a parent, now, but 24/7 can be a long haul when that time is filled with so much worry. I'm not sure that if I continued without a break like this that I'd be able to fully give Jake all that he needs from me. It is really important that I have this time to re-charge. I take this time to catch up with the household chores and my business, as well as some time with Brian and with friends, without the need to continuously check in with Jake. I know and trust that he is in very good hands and having fun with his brother. This arrangement is a great opportunity for Jake to see how it feels to be living in his new residence while attending classes. It's the next step towards him eventually living there without his brother shadowing his moves.

I have an easy drive back to the university on the Friday afternoon when I return to pick up Nick and Jake and bring them home for the weekend. They both look happy and they tell me that they have had an entertaining and productive week. I have no doubt that their week had been filled with much joy and laughter, as is usually the case when they get together. Jake attended all of his classes and lectures, some of which Nick sat in on. During their down time, when Jake didn't have homework assignments, they played table tennis. Jake met up with a couple of his friends from secondary school who also attend Guelph University, and made plans with one of them to start playing squash at the recreation center. He also attended a residence meeting, with the encouragement of his brother, but says that he didn't make any connections there. Nick makes jokes about how cold and uncomfortable the floor was, as he slept in a sleeping bag all week, and that we should all really have an appreciation for the sacrifice he made. His efforts during the week are definitely appreciated, in more ways than he can understand. Jake tells me that having Nick with him provided the momentum to do some of the things he hadn't been able to muster up the motivation to do on his own. Nick also provided another accountability factor that Jake now sees as so necessary to keep him going. He also mentions that he feels much less anxious, and that he would like to spend the following week on his own in residence. This moment is huge!

I'm willing to agree to give this a try next week and will re-visit the plan the following Friday to modify it, if necessary. Jake will still need to come home most weekends, as he continues to work part-time at the pub, and wants to continue to snowboard at the resort that is close to home. Although I feel quite nervous about it, I understand that I do need to give Jake the liberty and space to show me he is making strides in the work he's put into this semester, so far. It's important that he starts to feel that he has more control of things now and can begin to manage them on his own. Although this had become a situation so critical that I had to monitor and control it closely, I am careful not to have it overtake me, and become a jumping off point of paranoia and parental policing. I remind myself often that he is an adult, and if I push too hard, he can push back. The words "Helicopter Parent" hover closely in my mind, and I am very aware that my tendency to control too much can develop an out-of-control momentum. It is a time for me to take a leap of faith and show Jake that I believe that he is capable, and so I agree with his plan.

~~~~~~

It's still early February and this morning I manage to get both Jake and Nick to join me and participate in circuit training fitness class. Once again, I am in awe of the fact that both of my boys are easily comfortable in joining a class of middle-aged women and carrying on with their fitness goals as though it's a class of other young peers at a local gym. We have a great workout, go home and clean up, and then prepare to head to the city for the night. Jake is going to spend the night at Nick's apartment, so we drop the two of them off first. Brian and I carry on and check into a hotel for the night. It's a very special evening ahead for us, and it will be a matter of a few months before we realize just how extraordinary it really is. It is our friend Barb's 50th birthday celebration and she is gifting us with a private concert featuring the Canadian band Whitehorse to be held at the Rivoli Club.

Nick and Jake have grown up knowing Barb, and she has been an exceptional role model for them. Barb was a pretty typical teenager before her life was changed dramatically as the result of her being shot during a convenience store robbery, leaving her a quadriplegic at just eighteen-years-old. What this means is that Barb has no movement of her body from her neck down. She has the use of her head and makes good use of that very limited ability by using an electric wheelchair powered by a panel she controls with the back and sides of her head. She was twenty-six years of age when Nick was introduced to her, just a five-day-old baby who we brought to her home for her annual Christmas party in 1991. Barb had just defied all odds and graduated from the University of Arizona in journalism and was valedictorian of her graduating class the year previous. Jake was introduced to Barb when she was thirty and already an established journalist with the Toronto Star newspaper. As if it is not enough that my sons are fortunate as to be part of the life of a woman who shows tremendous tenacity, despite her physical challenge, it is the exceptional woman that Barb is in her day-to-day life that is so awe-inspiring. Barb works tirelessly as an activist and champions the issue of accessibility for the disabled; she speaks out about the need for medical marijuana, and she has created the Barbara Turnbull Foundation for Spinal Cord Research. She partnered with the Canadian Paraplegic Association to create the annual Barbara Turnbull Golf Tournament, raising more funds for spinal cord research. Barb has also been recognized with many awards, including the Steve Fonyo Medal of Courage, and the YWCA Woman of Distinction. Barb continues to write for the Toronto Star, and has also written two autobiographies, the first titled *Looking in the Mirror* and the second called *What I Know: Lessons from My 30 Years of Quadriplegia*. And she has been awarded not one, but two Honorary Doctorate of Law Degrees, from the

University of Toronto and York University. If I had one word to describe what Barb always teaches me and my boys, it is humility, for despite her having a very long list of accolades for her extraordinary efforts and work, Barb never flaunts these when she is around us. She is Barb, kind, generous, and fun, with an incredibly sharp wit, and who loves to host social gatherings, talk, enjoy music and great food, and most importantly, laugh with her family and friends.

Needless to say, celebrating 50 years of such a beautiful friend is an honour for my family and I, and we are looking forward to being a part of the evening. We each happily pay our cover charge, which is to be directed to Spinal Cord Research. Barb just never stops giving.

Brian and I meet up with Barb's sister, Lynn, to have dinner before the band begins, and then Nick and Jake join us a little later for the concert. It is a wonderful night of celebration and a reunion of many of the people I had met and spent time with during my time as Barb's attendant, as well as the friends we've made during Barb's many annual events, including her summer barbeque, Christmas party and house concerts. I decide at the last minute to take my camera with me, and soon realize that this is a night that needs to be fully captured in photos. I do my best to catch numerous digital images of the guests, the band, and of course, Barb enjoying a night of wonderful birthday memories. With all of the stress and worry over Jake's emotional state these past few months, it is great to have a night to forget all of that and just enjoy the moment. When the band finishes their encore the boys part company with us and head back to Nick's apartment. Brian and I remain in the city at a nearby hotel, agreeing that we will meet up again the next day for a family brunch. It's an absolutely memorable night and I am so happy to have shared in Barb's celebration.

~~~~~~

Jake and I are having a nice Monday morning at home, relaxed, and are watching another episode of Super Soul

Sunday. Mid-day we leave to return to the university. Jake is really excited about staying in residence on his own for the week. Nick helped him lay a good foundation for independence, reminding him to use his free time with more meaningful recreational activities. Now Jake is feeling a part of what it means to be a student and immerses himself into the whole experience. This time, on his own, is a great opportunity for Jake to make some more social connections, especially with the students in his residence pod. I'm not sure how much of an effort the others want to make, since they're well into second semester and likely have their own routine carved out. Just because they are sharing a common area doesn't necessarily mean that they will share anything in common. But, it's a good place to start. Jake has spent so much of his free time developing and nurturing his online friendships that I hope it doesn't create a crutch-like cushion for him. I do hope that he finds his way and creates friendships with other students while at school.

We agree that since I am not physically going to be at or near the university at all, and I have some of my own anxiety around this part of the journey, it would be most helpful if Jake takes a photograph in his classroom and lecture halls upon his arrival and forwards it to me via an email. Jake understands why this exercise in accountability is necessary, as he has not always been honest about whether or not he's doing what he says he's doing. He also wants to provide me with a sense of comfort while he works through a week of navigating on his own. It's scary for both of us but moving through the fear is absolutely crucial at this point for both of us to move closer to the end goal.

I drop Jake off at the residence, help him to lug in more of his personal items, hug him tight, and wish him well. I drive away feeling confident about our plan, and I want to believe in Jake's ability. It is clear by Jake's attitude of confidence that he feels determined that he's ready to make this work, and I need to support him. I leave him with the understanding that this separation may be difficult for both of us, but it's time for me to let go and give him the space and freedom to now give it his best attempt. He's well aware that I am just a text or phone call away, if it's not working out, and I have to hope that this time he reaches out sooner rather than later. As I often do, I say a prayer of gratitude for all of the wonderful systems that have been put in place both at home and at school to help Jake, and then promise myself to just surrender my worry. If I don't truly let go, if I hang on to my fear, then I am not truly practicing faith. For me, this exercise in faith is the only way to instill a sense of peace within. I drive on home.

The week is full of text messages, emails with classroom photos, and phone calls from Jake. This communication is just one more reason to appreciate what technology can now provide. In order to feel a sense of trust and peace, I can wait for a simple email with an attachment to arrive on my phone or desktop computer, and with a click on the attachment see the photo of Jake's class, and know that he's being responsible about his education. This transparency helps both of us enormously. He finds the evenings the hardest. He's still spending a lot of his time on his own. One evening he finds himself helping a friend with an assignment. He later tells me that while proofreading her work he was experiencing a lot of mental confusion and lack of focus, and just couldn't concentrate well. After a long period of frustration with his inability to fix his attention on the task, he eventually realized that he had forgotten to take his second dosage of his remedies for ADD that day. This is an important moment for Jake. I'd asked him a couple times before if he felt the remedy he was taking for ADD was helping, and he wasn't always sure how much it was. It was in not having it in his system that he recognized just how much it actually has been helping him to keep his focus. This realization is a positive sign and a good reminder for him to take the capsules more regularity.

Although Jake is good about sending photos from inside his classrooms and lecture auditoriums, as the week progresses I have a gnawing sense that outside of the classes he's struggling. He's only taking three courses, and his schedule is pretty light. That leaves a whole lot of empty, open space, and that can be dangerous for Jake, especially if he's feeling isolated and lonely. I don't say anything to him during our conversations because I want him to believe that he can handle this. I can't yet trust that he will confess any problems with me, as I don't quite feel the deceit is fully behind us. My being out of sight may give Jake a false sense of security. He now knows that I can see right through him in a lie, when we are together, and I will push him to be more honest. But away from me, he can pretend everything is good, and I am not there to challenge him.

In actual fact, what Jake is doing in private is not really my business. I tell myself that he's an adult now, which means that he has the right to make decisions without requiring my permission. He should now be capable of making his own choices, both good and bad, and face the consequences of his actions. He can have a fantastic week, disciplined in attending classes and completing school assignments, looking for and participating in social engagements, and come home feeling a sense of victory. Or he can stumble along, making not-so-good choices, spend far too much time online with friends, watching YouTube videos, and games, and avoid doing homework. Jake has to live with these choices, and it will only serve to provide him some very valuable information – he's either ready to triumph or he's not.

Ultimately, he will live with the consequences, and if unsound decision-making becomes chronic, then Jake will be required to make some hard decisions about his future, that will or will not include attending university and getting a degree. I believe that at this point I have provided enough evidence to him that I definitely have his back and am here to catch him if he falls again. But he has to ask now for that assistance before the tripping up becomes a catastrophe.

In part, my role in parenting my adult child is to step back, allow and encourage; the rest will be up to Jake. It seems simple enough in theory, but not always so easy to navigate. A mother always wants what's best for her offspring, and there's a fierce determination inside of her that wants to steer that ship, so to speak, in the direction she feels will be most beneficial. Mothers believe they always know what's best for their child, but when it comes to the course a young adult will take in getting there, a mother has no choice but to eventually give up the steering wheel. Surrender is necessary, but it's hard, it's so, so hard. Knowing when the time has come to completely let go is even harder. Is it now?

Chapter 27

It's Friday the 13th, and I suppose I could jump on the bandwagon and believe that my day is going to be full of bad spells and poor luck, but I don't. I am too excited to see Jake to start thinking negative thoughts. And even if I hear that Jake's week has been a disaster, I can't blame it on superstition. We're also dog-sitting for the weekend, so I have a young and frisky, ninety-pound Golden Labrador to keep me feeling cheerful. It's a wickedly cold day; starting at -30 degrees Celsius upon waking, and now a tepid -15. I am being facetious; the cold snap we've experienced so far this winter has been a blessing, for it has brought less snowfall, and enabled me to drive back and forth to Guelph on clear roads. Today the drive is easy, and I am able to enjoy the scenery. I have always loved the hue of the winter skies, an enthusiastic blue that awakens my visual sense, and sharpens the snowy landscape with a glistening sheen. I arrive early and get some shopping done in Guelph before Jake's last class ends.

Jake jumps into my Jeep at 5:00 p.m., his school week complete, and we make our way home. Today marks the beginning of Reading Week for the students and professors, and Jake says he's feeling a sense of relief in knowing that he gets this next week off from the obligation of school. As we drive, he also seems a bit down, to me. Generally, if he's trying to hide things from me, he's over the top enthusiastic and puts forth a front of confidence, and it always makes me suspicious. On this occasion however, he just seems a bit mournful and blue. I ask if he's taken his remedies, thinking that maybe he's forgotten it while being so focused on executing his first week independently at school. He says he's taken it and it's still helping, but that he had a difficult week emotionally. I invite him to share with me.

Jake explains that during the week that he was in residence with Nick, he'd heard that someone whose work he deeply respected and enjoyed had passed away suddenly at a young age. Jake tells me that he learned about it on the day that it happened but didn't believe it. He was waiting for something to appear online to say that it was a prank and that the man was still alive. And after a week passed he finally accepted that it wasn't a cruel joke, and the impact of the news hit him hard.

I learn that this man was Monty Oum, and that Jake had been, for the last two and a half years following some of his work, including his creations in Anime, which is a form of Japanese animation. Anime is huge in Jake's life and it's part of the reason he wanted to visit Japan and experience Japanese culture last year. On that trip, Jake bought and brought home with him several Anime figures, and he reads, watches, and follows this animation culture closely. Accepting the loss of one of the creators was an enormous blow to him.

Monty Oum was an American, self-taught, web-based animator who produced many crossover fighting video series, which involves non-stop animation action in a few short minutes. His style caught the attention of the Internet production company Rooster Teeth, who then hired him. He created custom animations for a series called Red versus Blue, and was best known for RWBY, a web-based Anime series, all created, written, and produced by Monty himself.[6]

On the very first day of this month, Monty Oum passed away at the young age of 33 after suffering an allergic reaction during a simple medical procedure which at first left him in a coma for ten days. He had a fan base so extensive and so loyal that many came together in their grief and helped to raise over $221,000 to cover the costs of his medical and funeral expenses.[7]

Jake was a loyal fan and idolized this man for his brilliant and very prominent work. And he found the loss to be devastating once he accepted its legitimacy. He explains to me that he had spent much of his down time during the week watching many of the videos of Monty's productions over and over, and sobbing, alone in his room.

I completely understand Jake's sense of loss. Although I didn't know Monty Oum and I didn't follow his career, I can empathize with the pain of this man's family; he died far too young, and it would seem that this was also a loss of immense talent in the entertainment world. I recall when I was pregnant with my first born, and close to my due date, learning that Freddie Mercury, lead singer of the band Queen, had died at age forty-six. I was so caught up in my world of pregnancy that I hadn't even known that he was suffering with the AIDS disease. My husband and I were cleaning up the basement much of that day, and I commented to him about the many Queen songs the radio was playing that afternoon. My husband then dropped the bombshell and told me that it was in honour of the loss of Freddie Mercury. I was devastated. The very first concert I had attended in my teens was a Queen concert. I was at an impressionable age, and I was quite captivated by the experience, immediately becoming an enthusiastic and loving fan. I didn't know Freddie personally, nor did Jake know Monty, but we really don't need to know someone intimately for them to have substantial impact on our lives. And once we saturate ourselves in their talent and their gifts, the veil of mystery disappears, and we feel a personal closeness, whether it is tangible or not. Clearly, Jake was having this experience, and I needed to offer understanding and compassion. If Jake skipped his entire week's classes to mourn the loss, it would have to be okay.

I don't want to take away this very real pain that Jake is

feeling for the loss of this man he so greatly admired. I also am very aware that he has needed to cry many tears, not just for this particular tragedy, but over the losses he had not yet grieved, like the death of his grandfather, and his dog, Thunder, and the loss he experienced during his middle school years when he felt isolated. He has buckets of tears to shed, and this loss became an outlet for Jake to fully express his feelings, rather than wrapping them up tightly inside. That dam he had described to me a few weeks ago, after hearing Timothy Shriver share his story, had finally burst, and that release had been granted. Although I feel so badly for Jake in his heartache, I am relieved to see that he has found the courage to express his emotional pain. This is a necessary part of Jake's healing journey, and I have a huge appreciation for him in sharing it with me. I know I am experiencing a moment of grace. I tell him that I understand, and in a gesture of empathy I reach out to touch his arm and give it a gentle squeeze. Nothing else needs to be said.

~~~~~~

    I spend Jake's Reading Week nursing a head cold, the result of the emotional strain of the last few months, I am sure. I receive an upsetting call early in the week from my dear friend, Marsha, who lives in Ohio. Her father has suffered a massive stroke, and the family has decided to remove him from life support. Within a couple of days, he passes away. Under any other circumstances, I would fly to my friend and give her support, but it's too critical a moment in Jake's recovery to leave him on his own, and in my condition, I am in no position to travel, nor do I wish to share my germs. I feel very badly that I cannot offer more than a few comforting words by telephone, but I also must recognize my limitations. I stay home and continue to monitor where and when I am needed; I get the rest I require and wait patiently for my energy to return and for this virus to exit. I say a prayer for Marsha and her family and tell her that I am just a phone call away if she needs to talk.

Jake spends his school break fully embracing winter, the snow, and the very cold temperatures. He is out on the slopes snowboarding for several days, both solo and with friends. He works at the pub on dishwashing duty a few nights, as well. These are two of the things Jake enjoys most: the freedom of flying down a snowy run, challenging his agility and skill, and immersing himself in the camaraderie and clattering chaos of a busy restaurant kitchen atmosphere. It is just the reprieve from school that he needs, and a good diversion to keep him from being tempted to play online video games. We talk about how it feels for Jake to be away from interactive online gaming, and although he has managed to stay free of it, he says that the desire is still deeply ingrained. He finds it difficult to not play, and he misses the online social interaction he had built, but he keeps telling himself not to give in to it. He understands it's no longer a healthy choice. There is some comfort in hearing that Jake has come to this understanding, but there is always an omnipresent sense of fragility, where at any moment Jake can succumb to this urge. That may never leave.

Footnotes:

[6]

https://en.wikipedia.org/wiki/Monty_Oum

[7] http://kotaku.com/rooster-teeth-animator-monty-oum-has-passed-away-the-p-1683287272

Chapter 28

The week ahead is an opportunity for Jake to remain on his own at school, but he inadvertently leaves a textbook at home that he needs, and then realizes that his cell phone is broken, so by mid-week I am needed for rescue. By weekend, Jake is home again and working a dishwashing shift and delighting in another day of snowboarding. Since the second semester began, I have encouraged Jake to start job searching for the summer. He has the option of looking for employment close to home, where I can drive him in, or in the city where he can bunk in with his brother and have access to public transit. He's been on summer job searches online and has sent out his resume, but has, as of yet, come up empty.

When we have time to talk I share with him a conversation I had with my friend, Gillian, earlier in the week. I was scrolling through Facebook and happened to notice that she had posted something in regard to her husband's new and growing tech company. There was a link to click for those who were interested in applying for a full-time position within the organization. I browse the link to see just what kind of employment position they were looking to fill. They want a full-time employee starting now, not a summer student. Something about it provokes me to send a private message and ask Gillian if her husband's company would be hiring students for the summer. I let her know that Jake is studying software engineering at Guelph U. Gillian replies immediately, and lets me know that she's unsure, but very kindly offers her husband's email address and suggests that Jake send him a resume with a cover letter. I pass this information off to Jake, encouraging him to not waste any time in making this connection, as many university students will have already applied for and landed their spring/summer jobs. I've stepped up and asked, and the ball is now in his court to proceed, if he wants to.

Jake returns to school the following week and must successfully manage to meet his class schedule and workload, and to sleep overnight in residence. He even meets with his professor to discuss next year's courses. Unfortunately, the co-op portion is no longer an option for Jake, but he is able to remain in the Computer Science Software Engineering program. This will shave off a year of school completion but denies him access to work placement and opportunities for future employment. Upon graduation he will be on his own in maneuvering his way into the job market. He tells me he's feeling fine about that decision. I am disappointed that this opportunity slipped through Jake's hands, but it is not the end of the world. Given the recent reality check I was stunned with regards to Jake's state of mind last semester, this decision by the university is not an enormous setback. As the week progresses, Nick also continues to communicate by text and emails with Jake, wanting to check in and track his movements, offering guidance and backing, as needed. That allows me to be able to relax a little more and focus on my own personal and business tasks. I am so grateful to have Nick's help. Diligent parenting can be a lonely process, and part of me wishes that Brian had more free time from his demanding work to be more of a help. But, as has always been the way, he has trusted me with much of the parenting role. His support in my decision-making allows me the freedom to make quick judgements, as they arise.

Jake and I meet again on Friday night and during the drive home from school I ask him if he's heard from anyone with regard to a job, and he tells me that Gillian's husband, Marc, has replied to say that Jake is not the person he is looking for in terms of the full time job position that was posted, but that he is passing along Jake's resume to the company's Chief Technology Officer (CTO) to see if he has any summer jobs available. Encouraging news!

Jake then tells me that, when I had first suggested he look at the company's job posting, he hesitated to go ahead and apply. After looking at the job link he saw that they were looking for a web developer type person who had experience in marketing and design. Web design programming and structure was a subject Jake had to take in both secondary school and then again in first year of university and it was definitely not his favourite. In fact, it was the very thing he hated. He also didn't feel confident that he had enough experience to work for this company, that the jobs were likely beyond his level of expertise. After thinking about it throughout that day, he then said to himself, "Essentially, I need a summer job, and no one else is calling me or replying to my applications, so what have I got to lose?" So, he sent in his application. I applaud him for taking this initiative and for being able to talk himself through it, free of my influence. This step shows progress.

Early the following week, I hear from Jake via phone, the news that he has now heard from Daryl, the CTO of Marc's technology company.

"He asked me in an email if I'm willing to either move to the city or commute to the company, if I were hired to work for the summer," Jake tells me.

"And how did you respond?" I ask, feeling hopeful.

Jake responds, "I told him that I already have a place to live for the summer and have a resume with that address, and then I offered to send that one to him."

When Jake originally applied to this company, neither he nor I had any idea where the company actually was; we had both assumed that since Gillian and Marc live just north of us, that perhaps the business was close to us, also. Now that we realize that it's in Toronto and that they are asking about moving or commuting, it becomes a much bigger deal. This job opportunity feels exciting for both of us.

By Thursday of that week, Jake receives another email from Daryl and he sends me a message saying that he is being asked to come in for an interview. Jake is so happy to finally be getting a response from one of the many job applications he's sent out, and especially one from a company based in software and technology. We discuss this opportunity, look at Jake's school schedule and decide together that the following Monday morning might work best. I can drive Jake to the city, he can sit through his interview, and then I can get him to Guelph for his first class, which doesn't begin until early afternoon. The interview is arranged, Jake is given the company's address, and he is super-stoked. He tells his brother about the offer and sends him the address. Before Jake can Google the company, Nick looks up the company's address online, and discovers that it is about a 15-minute walk from his apartment. How perfect is this? Something about it feels so in sync; I sense that it will all go really well for Jake. I immediately share the news with Brian, and the whole family is now anticipating the outcome with hope.

Jake spends another weekend at home, joins me at circuit training class, gets in some snowboarding, and works a shift at the pub. In between he works on school assignments. By now he has a really good handle on staying on top of his school work, and is navigating his academic workload like a pro. I now see enormous progress and maturity in his attitude about university. He continues to see his counsellor every other week, and in between he has visits with his assigned Special Needs Advisor. He says that he finds both of these regular meetings very helpful. I am starting to relax, and Jake is starting to feel more comfortable and self-assured.

~~~~~~

Monday, the day of Jake's summer job interview, and he and I are both overjoyed about it. Jake is also nervous, and I don't want to add to it by feeling anxious. To calm myself and stay grounded, I say a prayer to the universe, and then surrender my worry. In letting it go, I am accepting the outcome. And so far, this process has synchronized so perfectly, that I truly have a great feeling about it. I follow my instinct and completely relax into it. This release isn't always easy for me and has taken years of practice. I'm human and I sometimes allow worry to seep back in and create a space for feelings of apprehension. Today, I am determined to be strong for Jake.

Our conversation on the way to the city is relaxed and light. I tell Jake that he looks professional and that I love the clothes he chose to wear for the interview. I don't dwell on telling Jake how he should behave in the interview. That would be fruitless. I know nothing of the tech world and have no idea what kinds of questions Jake would be asked. And I haven't sat in a job interview in a thousand years; I would just come across sounding old and stodgy. Its 2015 and I am out of my element where this interaction is concerned. I've made the mistake before, of trying to guide Jake in areas where I am behind the times, and which inevitably results in eye rolling and exasperation. I stay clear of this, and just want Jake to feel he's capable of handling this himself, whether he actually feels it or not.

I drop Jake off in front of the company's office building. I do not want to be that parent that sits in the waiting room while my grown son meets with his potential future boss. I head on over to Nick's apartment, and I sit and read from a novel I'm presently enjoying. This book is called *Longbourn* and is written by Jo Baker. It's the classic story of *Pride and Prejudice*, but with a different spin. It is told from the servants' point of view. It's so interesting and possibly ironic that I would have my nose in this particular novel at this time. A rather appropriate quote by the author jumps out at me:

"Things could change so entirely, in a heartbeat; the world could be made entirely anew, because someone was kind."[8]

I hope this serves as a parallel for Jake and our family in this very moment.

I've told Jake to text me when he's finished his interview, and I'll come back to pick him up. I surprise myself and become completely immersed in the novel, never thinking about Jake or the interview, and I suddenly jump when my cell phone buzzes forty-five minutes later. It's a text from Jake.

I pick up my phone and it reads: "I GOT THE JOB!!!!!"

I am floored, and so, so happy for Jake. I ask, "Are you ready for me to come and get you?"

Jake replies, "No, I want to walk back to the apartment to see what the walking route will be like."

"Okay. Send a text to your dad and to Nick."

I want them both to hear it from Jake first. I know he will be bursting to share. Within a minute my husband sends me a text, "Jake got the job! Woo Hoo!"

"I know! How great is that?" I respond, big grin on my face, my eyes welling up with happy tears.

"Are you two now heading to Guelph?"

I tell him, "No, Jake is walking back from the interview to the apartment."

Brian replies, "I bet that his feet are not even hitting the ground."

We both understand what this means to our son, although we have no idea in what capacity he has been hired or what his job will actually be. But someone believes in him, enough to take him into their company for the summer, and that's what matters most right now. And he aced the interview, getting the job on the spot. That is something to be proud of.

Fifteen minutes later Jake flies through Nick's apartment door, and when he sees me he jumps up and down on the spot, pumping his fists and yelling, overjoyed, "I got the job, I got the job!"

I get up to give him a congratulatory hug, and Jake, in his elation, lifts me right up off of my feet and starts squeezing the life out of me. It's a magical moment for both of us after months of hard work, diligence, struggle, perseverance, and determination to turn what was once a tangled, chaotic storm into a well-deserved calm. We both understand so deeply just what this means; Jake has truly turned a corner in his ambitious plan to right a wrong and has been handsomely rewarded. Jake has found a good rhythm in terms of his schoolwork and now he's been granted a summer job.

We leave the apartment, climb into the Jeep, and are on our way to the university, both still reeling with joy. We talk about how lucky Jake is to have landed himself a job in a technology company, where he can put into practice some of what he has learned at university, and where he can gain experience and take what he has learned back to school in September. Jake tells me that he has to study and learn another coding language before starting this job, and he's somewhat anxious about that. But he's also willing to do whatever it takes to arrive at work in April and be ready to do what is required of him.

We're on the road for about a half hour, still joyfully chattering away, when Jake suddenly bursts into tears. It's an abrupt turn, but I immediately recognize that these are not tears of sadness. They are the tears of letting go. This moment is a culmination of overwhelming emotion for all of the suffering Jake has endured, and for all of the work that he has put into arriving at this place. He had essentially rolled up his sleeves of fortitude, just a few short months ago, and did what he needed to do, even when it was tough, even when he didn't want to and needed to be encouraged and prodded; he pushed through his fears and anxiety, and now he is able to see why and where it is all leading him. He is being given an opportunity, in the most meaningful way. It isn't just his family who are willing to take a chance in him and believe in his talent, capabilities, and his person; an outsider sees in Jake what we already know he possesses. That is more powerful than any praise or compliment we can ever give him. He has passed the job interview, he's done it all on his own, and he is now overcome with emotion. I pass him some tissue and give him a knowing pat on his back and tell him, "I understand, Buddy. I believe that you are being rewarded for all of your hard work, and you deserve every bit of it."

Consequently, it's a very good week at school. Jake is over the moon, and this is exactly the confidence booster he needs to give him the durability to get through the rest of this semester. Jake has the task ahead of him of choosing his courses for next year, and it will be important that he sign in and register on time. He decides, on his own, to schedule it into his phone, so that he won't have to re-visit the panic he experienced last year, and end up missing another cut-off date.

Later in the week I hear from Jake that he has successfully registered for year two, semester one, and we are both relieved. He also says that he's heard from his boss about his summer position, and he's been given his hours and salary. We'd planned a family vacation in late May and this may throw a curveball into our plan. I suggest that Jake be upfront and honest with the company, and ask if he would be allowed to have this time off. Jake tells me that he'd be willing to forgo the trip to keep the job, if needed. But, as it turns out, this isn't necessary, as the company grants Jake the time off. Things are moving smoothly, and Jake is in a really great place. The following day I retrieve Jake from university and deliver him to his brother in the city, so that they can attend a concert together that night. This will provide the venue and the entertainment for a celebration; the timing is superb. I relax and have my own inner celebration, as temporary as it may or may not be.

~~~~~~

On Friday, I am hit with news that shakes me up again. Just as I relax into the belief that Jake has a good handle on time management, I am shown that there is more work still to be done. Jake has been playing a video game on his phone lately, and I was fully aware of it. I expressed my disapproval of it, but he convinced me that it wasn't like the interactive, multi-player games and that he didn't have an urge to play it incessantly. I didn't really believe that, but I couldn't take his phone away, and I came up empty in knowing how to stop it. I somehow convinced myself that because it wasn't player interactive and I was only aware of him spending a little time on it during free daytime hours, that it wouldn't be all that harmful. So, I gave in and against my better judgement I ignored it. Foolish of me, given the evidence of Jake's recent past. But he had seemed to be so disciplined with school and had convinced me that he was well organized with projects and assignments. And as ridiculous as it sounds, I didn't want Jake to be angry with me for coming down hard on him for every little aspect of his life. He'd been monitored very closely for months now, and I was tiring of being the parental spy. I admit that I wanted a break, but I also wanted him to feel that I trusted that he knew what he was getting into. I am aware of the term "choose your battles" and this one I chose to relieve myself from. I cowardly took the easy way out. I did have the authority to insist on my rules, given that I was providing the foundation that Jake needed to get through the semester with full support. But I didn't.

In Jake's defense, he's choosing to be transparent, as I have asked him to be. He didn't need to confess to me and I am grateful that he has. On our drive home from Guelph he explains to me that he got in late from the concert last night, and instead of going to bed, he decided to play a game or two on his phone. I know with Jake it is never just a game or two, it is always several. He played until he fell asleep, with the game in his hand continuing to run, and draining his phone's battery. Consequently, his phone alarm didn't ring in the morning; he missed getting the bus back to school for his morning classes and didn't make it to an important lecture he needed to attend. He knows full well the mistake he's made, and he tells me that he has removed the game from his phone, making another promise to himself and to me that he will not play video games at all.

This incident is a huge lesson for both of us. I'm disappointed in Jake, and at the same time I understand his lack of self-discipline and his distractibility as a result of his ADD. At this point I have done some research, and I know how easily a person's brain can become obsessed with something they love, while they ignore mundane. Staying on task and having a regulated bedtime is something Jake has often struggled with, and it's difficult for him to turn his overactive mind off and just rest. So, I know why he has chosen to play late at night. He's just been to a concert where the music was loud and overly-stimulating to the nervous system. Coming down from that high into idle quiet is not easy. But there are certainly other methods of quieting one's mind, ones that do not require an electronic device. Jake is well aware of this.

My job is to guide Jake, help him make good decisions, but my job is also to show Jake how to make these decisions on his own. That job should have been completed by the time he reached adulthood, at least that's what society leads us to believe. For some children growing into adulthood, the ability to predict the consequences of their behaviour and make sound choices comes early, but I would hazard a guess that for just as many or more, it comes much later. After all, the frontal lobe of the brain, that controls this ability, is not fully matured until age twenty-five. These young adult brains are not always fully developed, and as parents, we need to take into account potential lapses in judgement and continue to monitor and give guidance. Add anxiety, depression and ADD to the pot, and it is a baking project in preparation stage, certainly not one that is fully-cooked.

I know that I could have chosen to come down hard and insist that Jake take that video game off his phone a few weeks ago, but I am beginning to see that Jake needed this scenario to play out so that he could recognize that he clearly still has an issue with his time management. My own temporary stumbling, as a parent of my adult child, has resulted in a painful but necessary blessing in disguise. I now need to leave Jake with the mess and allow him to figure out how he is going to make up for the class he missed; I am not cleaning it up for him, and he is not asking me to. I am angry, disappointed, and frustrated. Jake, meanwhile, feels guilty, remorseful, and scared. He was to hand in an assignment to that professor and missing the class could potentially lose him the assignment grade. It feels like two steps forward and three steps back; a fast-tracked journey that just a few days ago, starting with a fabulous job interview that put Jake on a platform of intense happiness, has turned into a downward spiral that brings him to his knees with regret and panic. Life unfolding at our feet: it doesn't always have to look pretty, but it can bring enormous lessons and opportunity for growth. It is time to move past the enormity of how each of us is feeling, pick ourselves up, dust ourselves off, and start again, with fresh eyes and new knowledge. It's not a disaster; it's not even tragic. It's an opportunity for both of us to see how we want to move forward.

Footnotes:

[8] Longbourn by Jo Baker, Random House Canada Publishing, copyright 2013, Chapter VIII, page 56, paragraph 3

Chapter 29

    The following week at school is difficult for Jake, and he makes some avoidable mistakes. He has a tough time staying on task with school assignments. It should by all accounts be easier for Jake to get his work done, now that he is not playing video games late into the night, but it creates the opposite result. Being at school full-time through the week, and only having a part-time course load, has resulted in Jake having far too much empty time to fill. I recall a conversation we had earlier this school term when he explained to me that when he's alone, he has a hard time turning off his brain, and so he looks for mindless things to do to temporarily shut it down. I understand this; I too have a brain that seems to be in chronic spin cycle. I try to turn it off by reading a book or watching a movie. Exercise and playing tennis help, too. Jake discovered that gaming and watching videos online provided this outlet, but he had then gotten locked into them and the hyper focus they demand, which ended up exhausting his brain. Jake has apparently been filling far too much free time with this game on his cell phone. I have suggested that he find other healthier things to fill his time with, but he has struggled to make this work on his own. I certainly can't attend recreational activities with him at school; that would be social suicide for him. He's tried to join clubs on his own, but the timing of these hasn't always worked out with his schedule. And because he essentially locked himself into his residence, away from social interaction in first semester, and he's coming home every weekend, it's a struggle to create friendships within a formal social structure. I really do feel for him, and I wonder if university life is ever going to feel "normal". For Jake, making friends and having healthy social outlets is definitely a big part of it, and one of the missing links right now.

Time management has never been Jake's strong point, and the next time we have a chance to talk, face to face, I ask Jake what he thinks is essentially his biggest issue in moving forward with more ease. Once again, I am blown away by his candor.

Jake replies, "It's really hard. I just don't want to do all of the work; I'd rather just play."

"That's the most honest thing you've told me through all of this," I say. "I have days when I feel exactly the same way. Everyone does. There are times when I know that laundry and housekeeping, or office paperwork is waiting for me, but I'd much rather grab my tennis racquet and go play some doubles or arrange lunch with a friend. Working all of the time is tough, and not making time to play makes it even harder."

Jake seems pleasantly surprised by this, and I continue, "There comes a time when one understands that grinding through to get the work done, can be rewarded eventually with play time. This kind of thinking comes with maturity. There will always be those tasks that aren't our favourites, and can be downright boring, but they have to get done. It's really about finding a balance. This lesson is not one that I can teach you; it's something you will, over time, figure out how to manage, yourself."

My role in this moment is to let him know that I completely understand, and I appreciate his frankness. I tell him that what he is experiencing is completely "normal". I hope it helps, and only time will tell.

It is at this time that I start to consider writing about Jake's story. There have been so many ups and downs, so many twists and turns, so much learning. And as I have evolved through it, I have had several conversations with other mothers, mostly friends, family members, and some of those in my business network circle. The overall theme seems to be the same for everyone, and the question remains: How do we transition from parenting our child to parenting our adult child? And how do we meet their individual needs, especially during times of crisis? I seem to have started the conversation, in my quest to seek answers, but like me, every mother seems to be just blundering along, and trying to sort it out as it presents itself. No one seems to have the answers, and up until now, no one seemed to be talking about it either. I feel it may be time to put it down on paper, in the form of a story, and create an opportunity for both reflection and dialogue. I know that it is not just an issue for mothers; fathers can feel the same helplessness in this phase of parenting, but so far I have spoken mostly with women. We need to talk about this parenting transition. Awareness needs to be created so that we can formulate a healthier framework in which to move forward. We, as parents, are responsible for digging deep inside and awakening to an understanding of what it will take to shift from a momentum of constant supervision and management to one of facilitating independence, even after the age of consent. No easy feat, but a necessary one.

~~~~~~

Jake has finally been assigned a peer support student who will check in with him as needed. It would have been ideal to have this in place sooner, but as it requires a student volunteer to step away from their own workload, it's not an easy system to arrange. Better late than never, and after the last couple of weeks, with Jake missing classes and losing focus, the timing couldn't actually be better. Jake is now down to the wire with finishing assignments and then preparing to study for final exams, so it's key that he remains fixed on completing his three courses. Having an older student to mentor him and help him to organize his time is greatly appreciated now. Jake tells me he finds the meetings are very helpful.

It's great that Jake has another set of eyes checking in on him to provide a strategy for helping him reach his school targets. It turns out that I have been invited to a family wedding which will take place in Punta Cana, Dominican Republic, at the beginning of April. Iris's daughter, and Barb's sister, Christine, is marrying her sweetheart, Ron, and because the family means so much to me, I have also offered to take the wedding photographs, as my gift. I haven't photographed a wedding before, I have done mostly professional headshots, and a few family photos, but I am quite excited about this project. Photography has been a hobby of mine for quite some time, and over the last few years it has begun to develop into a small business. This wedding will be a great experience to test and expand my creativity. Weddings would normally be far more pressure for me than I'd be willing to take on, but this will be a small and casual affair, and I feel completely comfortable in offering. Having said that, it's still extremely important for me to do a really great job and capture the essence of the day and their love for one another. I am quite excited about this opportunity and am thrilled to be a part of this family occasion.

I am also anxious about leaving Jake on his own, but by the time I will be on the airplane to leave for the Dominican Republic, Jake will be on his last two days of classes and lectures, after which Brian has agreed to step in and bring him home until exams begin. I assume that I will have Internet connection at the resort, and that Jake can stay in touch with me, if required. It is not just that I am concerned about Jake completing his year and assignments; I worry also that once he is home and without my supervision, he may be tempted to fall back upon excess video gaming again. I know that I need and deserve this break. It would have been nice to have Brian come along with me, but he can't get the time off work, and I need to have his all-important parental guidance in place for Jake so that I can feel a sense of calm.

I leave early in the morning for my trip, with wedding clothes, bathing suit, and my camera equipment in tow. I am happy but nervous to be temporarily saying good-bye to all of my responsibilities at home, and to enjoy some sunshine and heat with friends. Not all of Christine's sisters are able to make the trip, but Mom, Iris, Lynn, and Alison and her family join us. Sisters Barb and Chella are unable to travel at this time. Ron's sons are also along, as well as another family friend, Sue. It's a nice small group and Ron and Christine make a concerted effort to have us spend as much of our time together as possible during the five days. We eat breakfast and dinner as a group, play beach volleyball and tennis matches, as well as spend time at the resort's waterpark. I learn on the first day that Internet reception is poor and decide to surrender all of my concerns to Brian, back home, and allow myself this much needed reprieve. It's a challenge at first to let go, but as I realize how cathartic this break could be for me, I soon succumb to the heat and sun and absolutely no maternal responsibilities. The wedding is beautiful, and I enjoy, immensely, the opportunity to photograph the entire event. It's so unbelievably nice to be away, that the thought of going home so soon is a tad depressing for me. However, the short trip comes to an end and I'm soon returning home. I arrive late at night at the airport in Toronto and am greeted by both Jake and Brian. It's really nice to see them but feels strangely unfamiliar to be home already. The trip just seemed to be a blur of activity and fun, a bit of a whirlwind, and some beach vacation fantasy. The days passed far too rapidly. Now, back to my responsibility as a wife and mother again.

Chapter 30

Exam day comes, and Jake tells me that after studying all weekend for this first test, he feels well-prepared to write it. I drive him to Guelph. We park at the university, and then part ways. I have been spending so much time at the university for the past few months that I know my way around easily. I head straight to the coffee shop with a new laptop I recently bought, while Jake heads off to take his exam. I am finally able to start writing, and I am beginning to work on a book about Jake's story. My previous writing experience has only been in creating health newsletters and articles. This challenge is a much larger endeavor, but I push forward and begin. Over an hour later, Jake returns, exam completed, and feeling positive that he did well. We pack up and set off for home; one exam down, two to go, and a book begun.

The wedding party has now returned from the Dominican, and the following day I receive an early morning phone call from Iris's daughter, Alison, that leaves me feeling gob smacked. Yesterday, as the wedding party returned home from Punta Cana, Christine received a message and learned that Barb was rushed to hospital with some breathing issues and is now in an intensive care unit (ICU) and on a respirator. Only family are allowed to visit, so although I have an intense urge to get in my Jeep and drive straight to the hospital, I cannot. I want to be with the family, as I am certain that it is not only frightening for them, but also a nightmarish flashback to 1983 when Barb was shot and lying in ICU on a ventilator. I immediately share the news with Jake that Barb is unwell and in hospital, but I don't tell him how badly her prognosis is, as I do not want to upset him while he is still preparing for exams.

I am shaken and am feeling immense sadness, and I don't feel hopeful about this situation. I have always clearly understood that with the seriousness of Barb's spinal cord injury, her life expectancy would not be the same as an able-bodied person. And I have always had an acute awareness that each passing day with Barb is a gift that none of us should take for granted. I fear that this incident could take Barb completely out of our lives here on earth. The thought just tears me up, and for the remainder of the day I spend my time at home feeling utterly numb, trying to shut out my fears.

I eventually manage to start the photo editing process with Christine and Ron's wedding pictures, a work activity that always fills me with joy and satisfaction. But for today I just go through the motions, carrying a heavy heart. I am constantly waiting for my phone to ring with more news of Barb, but the day and evening passes and there are no more calls.

Days pass and I feel physically-isolated from the situation of Barb and her family. I understand and respect the rules that allow only family members into ICU, but coming from a five-day, amazing wedding vacation and spending so much time together, I feel abruptly separated. I am grateful for the texts and phone calls, and I am certainly kept in the loop, but I have this innate urge to hug and hold each and every family member in person. In the interim, I hold them in my heart and in my prayers.

Jake writes a second exam, feels he did well, and now has several days ahead of him to study and prepare for the next and final test of this semester. We spend another day at the skydiving simulator. I think this activity has got to be a great stress reliever for Jake at this point. Skydiving isn't something I am interested in, but I can imagine that having the ability to just hang above a strong air current and get so close to the feeling of flying, has got to be tremendously freeing, both physically and mentally. Spending this activity time with Jake feels like a bit of a celebration. Even though he's not quite finished with all of his school courses, it's close enough. We're down to the wire, and I am certain that he will meet all expectations for this term.

During the week, as I am journaling, I notice my notes from one year before, on April 11th. I was feeling so immensely happy that day, as I was helping Jake pack up the contents of his residence dorm room for the move back home. With total confidence I had believed that Jake had completed his year, without any issues, and was coming home to look for summer work and prepare to return for year two. Wow, how more wrong could I have been? What blinders was I wearing then? How little did I know of the inner sufferings that Jake was enduring, and how little was I doing to help him? Even though I was unaware of his predicament, I was somehow enabling it by not paying closer attention to the signs. I know now that he didn't want me to fully see it, but he'd certainly dropped some clues, and I somehow justified them all. Was it up to me to probe more deeply at that point? Or was it solely his responsibility as an adult to ask for help? This predicament is the blurred line I am always faced with, as a parent, and it's one I often wish was so much clearer. Where do we draw the line between letting go and allowing, and perhaps digging and snooping further into our adult children's lives, looking for clues that they are not really okay?

My focus shifts back to the now, and I write in my journal today that I am truly grateful at just how far Jake has come. He has worked really hard on both his emotional and physical health, with a better diet and a fitness regime. He has kept up with his counselling appointments, and he has worked hard at studying and applying himself in school. Coping with anxiety and ADD is a lifelong journey, and with healthy skills, ample support, and appropriate tools it can be managed well. Jake is proof of this.

Days later I manage to complete the wedding photo editing, eventually feeling able to enjoy the process again. I learn that

Barb is stable and hearing the news that she will be able to come off of the respirator soon has calmed my own concerns. My hope is restored again. Jake still has a few more days before his last exam, so we take time to start packing up some of his things to move him to his brother's apartment. Knowing how much the boys love to eat barbequed meat, my husband and I decide to treat them both to a new barbecue for Nick's backyard. It's not expensive but will be fine for their needs. Nick meets us at his apartment at the end of his workday, and we get right to the barbecue assembly. We bumble our way through the instruction manual, have a few giggles as we make a couple of mistakes, and eventually have it set up and ready to use. The three of us enjoy a dinner of grilled chicken and vegetables, and the guys look forward to enjoying many more meals together this spring and summer. I feel a sense of relief that Jake has now landed on his feet again. And I know that Nick will provide some of the stability that Jake needs. But a new journey begins, and I worry about whether or not Jake will be able to manage the responsibility of his own self-care as well as his new summer employment.

~~~~~~

    Its mid-April and a glorious day! The sun is shining brightly and the high for the day is 18 degrees! I am starting to see many of my garden perennials sprouting up to say hello. But the best part of the day is that I receive the news that Barb has successfully come off the respirator and is beginning to recover from pneumonia. We can all express a deep sigh of relief. As spring encourages new plant life, this news helps to breathe new life into all of us.

Two days later and Jake completes his last exam for semester two. He feels extremely pleased at what he has accomplished. We immediately get to work packing up the remaining personal items from his residence and head for home. We are both feeling in a celebratory mood. There has been so much personal growth for Jake these past six months, and he leaves school seemingly a very different person this year than he did after year one. Brian returns home from work for the weekend and we have a congratulatory dinner together.

The following day Jake moves into his brother's basement apartment, sets up his bedroom, and prepares to begin the next chapter. In a couple of days, he will be working with the tech company just around the corner, and he is both nervous and excited about this awesome opportunity.

Although Nick and I have gone over Jake's difficulties regarding time management, I don't want to burden Nick with micro-managing Jake's life. He's aware that his brother can be easily distracted and might forget to set his alarm on his phone, and he knows that Jake is not a great morning person and can be a bit muddled when it comes to organizing his day. I don't want Nick to feel like a babysitter, but at the same time I am really glad that Jake is not living entirely on his own anymore. I do need Nick to keep an eye on things and steer Jake in a positive direction, if needed, but more than anything my hope is that he will serve as an excellent role model. I recognize that Jake has been leaning on me as the person he was most accountable to, and I know that I will eventually need to wean myself from this role. It truly is up to Jake to make this work, but I have to admit that I'm not feeling a hundred percent confident in letting go just yet.

On Jake's first day of work I send him a text to say good morning, and to relieve my own worry about whether or not he's gotten up and is readying himself. Now I am most certainly feeling like a helicopter mom, and I feel guilty. At this point I should back away and allow Jake to take full responsibility, but instead I tell myself that it's temporary, and until I feel comfortable or Jake tells me to stop, I'll carry on as is. Some habits are hard to break, and I have been in a role of close supervision for months now. I want to feel confident in Jake's ability to manage his time and responsibilities, but his recent history allows for some doubt. Receiving a reply text helps me to relax and know that he's on his way to work.

For now, Jake seems cool with my checking in, and tells me

he's up and ready to go, and looking forward to his first day. I can now get on with my own day, and not worry at all about how Jake will handle himself on the job. That part I am completely comfortable with, for I know that Jake has what it takes to work hard and work well in this job environment. I have evidence of this from Jake's previous work at the pub. He became known and appreciated for his integrity and for getting along well with staff.

I relax into my day and get on with work, but it's not long before I receive some shocking, sad news.

My Uncle Tom has passed away.

I was not expecting this.

He'd had open heart surgery a few years back and seemed to be doing very well. He was such a huge and fun part of my childhood. Uncle Tom was always a man I enjoyed being around, as he was silly and playful. It was in those joyful moments in his presence that I could forget the oppression and anger surrounding me in my childhood home. When my Uncle Tom, Aunt Jean, and their children arrived to visit with us we all seemingly relaxed. I had learned through experience that my parents could put on happy hostess faces and their behaviour would become much more agreeable to my brothers and I. My mom's brother, Tom, was a fun-loving character whom our entire family adored. He told us kids off-colour jokes that no other adults would dare to tell, and he often brought out his guitar at family reunions and sang hilarious tunes. He had suffered a back injury that left him wearing a brace, and we were always reminded to be careful around him. And although he was the kind of guy you'd want to rush in, hug, squeeze, and joyfully climb all over, we instead enjoyed his presence from a close distance, careful not to further exacerbate his back problems.

Uncle Tom had a farm and I would happily agree to visit on summer weekends. It was during these visits that I was free to roam through the barns and enjoy the animals, and play with my cousins, Paul, Daryl, and Karen. It was during a summer holiday at the farm that I learned to ride a bicycle, and it encouraged me to return home and save my allowance to eventually purchase a bike of my own. That bike brought me a welcome sense of freedom, as I rode all over town, escaping the volatility in my family home. I would never forget that wonderful gift of the many visits with my Uncle and his family. My aunt Jean passed away with cancer, far too young, and quite a number of years ago Tom moved to the west coast and eventually re-married. I had a lovely visit with him and his second wife during my last trip to B.C.

Upon hearing the news of his passing, I learn that my mother has not been informed, yet. Apparently, Tom had known he was dying and had requested that his wife be discreet and that no one was to know. He wanted it all kept hush hush, and he didn't want a fuss made over him with any funeral preparations, either. Tom was my mother's last surviving sibling and they were close. Just a few years ago it was my mother who had sat by his bedside at the hospital as he was recovering from open-heart surgery. She deserves to know that he is gone, but I hate to be the one to have to tell her. I know that she will be very upset. I make the call, and the two of us cry and talk, attempting to comfort one another as best we can. There are no travel arrangements to make and I will not be flying to BC for the burial. And although the news of death is final, this one brings no sense of closure for either one of us. The best that we can do is to reach out to Tom's immediate family and offer our condolences. And so, we do.

It seems so unfair that just as things are unfolding with more ease I would be hit with this terrible loss. But that is life; we cannot stop its unfurling, and meeting each experience and challenge provides an awareness and a reminder of the fragility of each moment.

At the end of the day Jake calls to tell me all about his first day's experience at his new job. He is very happy with his day. He enjoyed meeting his co-workers and learning what his first project will be. His voice is filled with exuberance. This new journey is beginning well.

Every day for the next week I start my morning by sending a text to Jake, wishing him well. And at the end of the day he sends a text relaying to me all of the exciting new things he's learned, and to tell me how much he loves his new summer job.

~~~~~~

Now that I am not playing chauffeur for Jake, I have much more time to focus on myself, my work, my grieving, and on my relationship with my husband. We are now essentially empty nesters, free of parenting, for the most part. When our boys lived at home and we were responsible for nurturing and caring for their needs, they were required to fit into our lives. We made up the schedules and family events and they followed along. Now that they are both living away from home, we get to create a plan for just the two of us, just as Nick and Jake get to plan for their individual lives. We now wait to see how we fit into their adult lives. I know that room will be reserved for all of us to get together, and in the meantime Brian and I begin to transition into this stage. I am gentle with myself and I exhale some.

While Nick and Jake have their first weekend as roommates to play in Toronto, I finally have the opportunity to visit Barb in the hospital. She's off of the respirator, out of ICU, and now in a regular room. It is so great to finally be able to see her, but she's not having a particularly great day. It is the first time since I've known Barb that she appears vulnerable and fragile. The moment is bittersweet, a mixture of relief and concern. I leave the hospital feeling satisfied that I was able to spend some time with my dear friend, but I am concerned about her recovery.

It is just a matter of a few more days and then Barb will be released from hospital to continue her recovery at home, where she will still require oxygen and will need constant care. The family begins to organize around-the-clock assistance for her, and I offer to take a first shift.

It's now May and I've spent much of my weekend preparing my gardens for spring, plucking out weeds and edging the soil. I clean up and ready myself to spend the night at Barb's condo, as I have taken on the night shift. It means that I will literally be sleeping in the same bed with Barb, in order to be available, as she needs my assistance. The last time we slept in a room together was back in the early eighties when we travelled on vacation, and I was her attendant. This feels different, yet familiar; I am now temporarily in the role of caregiver once again.

I arrive at Barb's condo late afternoon. Her mother, Iris, has been staying with Barb full time since her release from hospital, but tonight she is returning to her home, and she wants to drive before dark, so I am gifted with a few extra hours to spend with Barb before we both go to sleep. Everything about this time feels so familiar to me; like riding a bicycle again, I fall into personal attendant mode with ease. But I remind myself that I am not just her caregiver, I am her friend, and this time helping Barb is my gift to my companion of many years.

Barb is really weak, her breathing seems laboured, and her throat is perpetually dry from chronic mouth breathing from her sinus congestion. I am mostly keeping her company, bringing her drinks of water, and applying lip-gloss to prevent them from chapping. We manage to have a lovely a visit, and I am so happy to be with Barb, even though she isn't well. I just want to give her any kind of comfort that I can muster.

As a quadriplegic, Barb requires attendants to get her undressed and ready for sleep, and to transfer her from her wheelchair into her bed. I have done these duties in the past, but not for many years. So much about Barb's personal care routine has changed, and I am out of that loop. Her night-time attendant arrives, a young woman in her twenties. She reminds me of myself at that age, when I worked for Barb. For a brief moment it feels like I am being taken on a journey into my past. The attendant gets to work helping Barb get ready and into bed, and then she brings me into the room and shows me what will be required for the night.

It is a long one, with much interrupted sleep for both of us, as I tend to Barb's needs. In the morning I am awakened by the arrival of the daytime shift. I shower and get dressed, and then it's time to say to good-bye.

Barb asks, "Did I wake you up a lot?"

"Yes, you needed my help several times, but that's okay. Your comfort was important."

"Thank you for everything. The next time I see you I will be better," Barb says, with a little smile.

"You're welcome," I say, and then lean in and kiss her on the cheek to say, "Good bye".

I drive away feeling like the entire time I just spent with Barb was like a full circle moment. It was truly a gift. Years ago, I never wanted to stop being her attendant because it was such a great time in my life, filled with fabulous memories of times spent with this amazing woman. A split second changed the course of life for both of us. That horrendous night when Barb was shot created a life of entrapment within her own body, and eventually led to us crossing paths just two years later. What began as a working relationship grew into a friendship spanning thirty years. It is an honour to be taking care of Barb again, but an even greater honour to call her my friend. Seeing Barb in this weakened condition, I am reminded of how grateful I am for all of the years that I could enjoy her company in good health. I say a prayer for her recovery and look forward to more days with Barb, and hope that she will be well again soon.

Jake is now over two weeks into his new job and is making great strides. He tells me that he has been given a programming project for the summer, and he has completed it in just over two weeks. His boss and co-workers are impressed. This accomplishment has been an enormous boost to his confidence, and creates an opportunity for him to be given even more responsibility. He also feels at this time that my morning text messages are no longer required. He tells me he understands why I needed to check in; he knows it was to relieve my concerns, but he would now like me to let go and trust him. This need for detachment actually comes as a huge relief to me. After months of close contact and constant accountability check-ins, I am now being fully released from my duties. Jake is taking the reins of responsibility back. I actually feel okay with this, but most likely, if I'm being honest with myself, it's because I know that he has his brother to lean on. My parenting is on hold, for now.

Mother's Day is fast approaching, and Nick and Jake are planning to come home to spend it with me. Time with my boys is the best present that they could give. I never want a bought-gift or flowers. I simply want to spend quality time with my sons. I look forward to our day together. I will also be driving the two of them back to Toronto on the Sunday night, after dinner, so I offer to take another night shift with Barb. Her condo is not that far to drive to from Nick's apartment. It will be both convenient and a pleasure to spend more time with my good friend.

Chapter 31

Today is Mother's Day, and I wake feeling so happy to have both of my sons at home with me. I can hear the guys, busy in the kitchen preparing a special breakfast. I walk downstairs and am given my cup of coffee to drink in the living room as they continue to cook. I bring my cell phone with me, a habit developed as a result of Jake needing me as a lifeline in the past several months. And since Barb has been so ill, I check it even more regularly. I open it to look for this morning's messages, and there's a text from Barb's sister, Lynn. I read it in absolute disbelief.

It reads, "Barb went into cardiac arrest at 10:00 p.m. last night and suffered catastrophic brain damage. It is unlikely that she will survive. Will keep you posted."

I scream like a fatally-wounded animal, and then burst into hysterical tears.

Nick, Jake, and Brian all rush into the room asking, "What's wrong?" I can barely catch my breath. I share the horrendous news between gasps of shock and horror. Immediately, we are all hugging and sharing in this jarring news, deep in our sorrow.

Although it was clear that Barb was still struggling to recover from the pneumonia and the weeks on the respirator, none of us saw it culminating in this tragic moment. We're all stunned and deeply saddened by the news. Our day will now be spent waiting to hear news of Barb's inevitable passing and celebrating Mother's Day now takes on a more somber tone.

Mid-afternoon my cell phone rings and I know what's coming. My heart sinks before I answer. It's Barb's youngest sister, Alison.

"Barb is gone," she tells me, and I erupt into tears.

"We were all together, gathered around her hospital bedside, playing music and sharing stories, and then Barb passed peacefully while listening to Neil Young," Alison tells me through her own tears.

"I am so sorry," is all that I can muster. The call is brief, and Alison says that she will be in touch again soon.

I am thoroughly broken-hearted at the news and I feel an enormous void. I feel so badly for Barb's mother and her sisters who are left behind to deal with their massive grief and loss. I can tell Brian, Nick, and Jake, are feeling their own personal pain. Barb is gone. It's so hard to absorb this truth. I honour the loss and I take the time I need to feel my sorrow. I spend my afternoon shedding more tears. This release is only the beginning; grief comes in waves over time. I also need to find a space to appreciate the woman that Barb was and the many wonderful memories she has left in my heart. I am so grateful for the time that I spent with her last Sunday; I see now it was an incredible gift. It helps to ease some of the pain. I have closure in that special time that we shared. Neither of us knew it then, but we were already saying our good-byes.

We make the best of Mother's Day and take comfort in each other's presence. I think of Iris often through the remainder of the day, and the cruel irony of this day. As a mother, my heart aches for her. I can't even imagine the pain and sorrow she must now carry.

After dinner I take Nick and Jake home, and we part knowing

that we will be together again very soon to attend Barb's funeral. It has been a bittersweet day.

~~~~~~

    The following week my heart feels heavy, and the house feels too quiet and empty during the day. Selfishly, I wish that Jake was still living at home, so that I wouldn't be so alone with my grief. I find myself immersed in reading online news articles about Barb's passing. I gather together and send some of the photographs I had taken of Barb to her family. They will use these, along with many others for a memorial slide show. I search the online archives and watch videos of Barb speaking at formal events that she had participated in, much as Jake did upon accepting the loss of Monty Oum. I am reminded of her remarkable intelligence and wisdom; I revel in the sound of her voice and her laughter and her light sense of fun that shines through the screen. And I cry. The world has lost a bright light, but not before she left her unmistakable mark. Barb was an outstanding individual who did more with her life to create positive change and open doors for many, than most able-bodied individuals have ever done. I am filled with many great memories, so many unbelievably awesome moments, and I feel extremely blessed to have known Barb, and to have called her friend.

I worry about Jake. He is sensitive and feels so deeply, and it is only recently that he has begun to fully express the grief he'd locked up inside for years. He's just begun such a wonderful new path, and I pray that this loss doesn't steer him down a darker one. I also hope that he will find a way to release his sorrow. I know that he loved Barb deeply. Nick seems to be able to compartmentalize loss in his own way, with an inner knowing that this is the way life shifts and moves, and he seems to be able to make peace with that. Nick will keep his feelings to himself and show an outer strength. I'm never sure what is locked up in there, but in the past, he has shown that he can handle sad news with a strength that helps him endure it. I have never sheltered him or Jake from death or funerals. Jake has always been more fragile with his feelings, while Nick comes across as strong and able to handle loss with grace and acceptance. He may at times try to be stoic, but I believe he understands that I always have a shoulder to lean into, if ever he needs one. Brian too is sensitive, but he wears his emotions on his sleeve. I have always appreciated that in him. We can cry together unabashedly, even if it's over a sappy television commercial or a sad movie, passing one another a tissue with full awareness that our tears are a necessary release. He is both strong and soft at the same time.

The following weekend we attend the funeral for Barb, which is held in a large cathedral in Toronto. There are five hundred in attendance, all paying their respects to someone who made a difference in their lives, big and small. We are invited to sit in the front pews of the church, along with family and close friends. We feel honoured by this request. More importantly, we want to be within range of providing our support to Barb's mother and her sisters. It is a beautiful, touching tribute, with speakers and singers who pay homage to Barb's life with their words and their music. The heartfelt words and angelic songs produce an aura of divinity in the cathedral. We attend the very moving burial service at the cemetery, and then a private reception at an estate close by. There are more speeches, but there is music, always music; Barb loved music. Jake is emotional and it is clear that he has been deeply affected by the loss. I breathe a small sigh of relief amid my own tears to see him express his anguish and accept the comforting embraces from those around him. As much as I want to protect and shelter him from his grief, his expression of tears shows great strength and a willingness to face this loss and not bury it. It is an immensely sad day for all of us. It is also a day of celebration for a life in which each of us is so very proud to have played a part.

Chapter 32

A new week begins, and the numbness slowly begins to dissipate. The reality of Barb's parting leaves me with a heavy, nauseous feeling in my stomach. There will be no more visits to Barb in her condo, no more of her house concerts or dinners together, and she will not be in attendance at her annual summer barbeque, which we have decided to continue. We had thirty years of friendship and I still want more. Now, the process must begin to move forward and I'll need to get on with my day-to-day living, but with such a heavy heart. My life has been touched in such a way that I will never feel the same again. I am hungry, and yet full.

At the end of the month we leave for a family trip. At the time that we planned this journey we had no idea just how much it would be needed. This holiday is a time to bond together privately, to take a temporary break from the somber reality of loss, to pause and create something new and meaningful. Traveling together on vacation is good medicine for our family.

We fly to Paris, France to begin an eight-day adventure exploring new territories. Our family has travelled together many times since Nick and Jake were very young. The guys have always navigated each journey with ease, like it is second nature to them. Interestingly, our last trip with the four of us together was our journey to Barcelona, Spain just a few short days after we'd quite unexpectedly lost our little dog, Thunder. And although the timing was not good, it did set the tone to begin the healing process. Grief is very hard on the body as well as the psyche and being able to take this time to relax and self-nurture is definitely a gift. As time goes on, and Nick and Jake paired off with partners and then families of their own, our family-of-four vacations will be a thing of the past. So, I appreciate this opportunity all the more.

The initial plan for our holiday time was to have it split between time spent as a family, some couple time for Brian and I, and time for Jake and Nick to explore on their own. Unexpectedly, we share more of it all together. We also divide the trip between France and Belgium. After landing in Paris, we rent a car and drive to Ypres. We share a large rental home, and travel by car through the countryside to visit many of the war memorials and cathedrals and devour some amazing Belgium waffles and chocolates. In contrast, when we return to Paris, we rent an apartment downtown and opt to use the transit system and do more walking. Brian and I attend the French Open for a day, which was on our personal bucket list. We'd like to eventually see all of the tennis grand slams around the world. We also have a night at the opera, which is something I enjoy, and that we haven't done in a number of years. Brian and I have both been to Paris before, but never together. This trip to Paris is a first for Nick and Jake, so they spend their time exploring much of it on their own. Visiting Belgium is a first for all four of us.

We return home several days later, feeling refreshed and ready to carry on with routine. Nick has a business trip and must turn around and fly to New York the next morning, and Jake will return to his summer job. There's very little time to worry about jet lag until the weekend arrives in a couple of days, and then we can all crash and try to catch up on sleep. I spend some much-needed time in my gardens, as spring is now upon us, and there is still so much to get done. I organize an annual garden party each year in June, and it's important to me that our property looks well-tended and inviting for my guests. I accomplish much in a few short days and then feel quite exhausted. Lucky for me, the spring rain comes, and I get a few days reprieve.

~~~~~~

Upon my return trip from Europe, I get a message from Iris, asking me to call her. I worry that something is wrong and call back immediately. Iris assures me that everything is fine. She has had a conversation recently with her daughter, Lynn, and it was suggested to her that she take on a houseguest in her new home. She knows that Jake attends school in Guelph, where she lives, and she thinks he would be a wonderful guest. She even offers to cook for him. She is also well aware of the difficulties Jake had last year, and for me the idea of Iris providing her home, her food, and her lovely company might be just the support that Jake needs to have a better start to his full year of school in September. Iris is still mourning the loss of her daughter, and I worry that this may be too much for her. She assures me that it will be okay. Perhaps having company in her home will help her to cope a little easier. The invitation sounds perfect for both Iris and Jake! But of course, it is the mother in me who wants something that sounds so good for Jake. I know that he adores Iris and her family, but I'm not sure that he would prefer this living arrangement to returning to residence. I know what I would choose for Jake, but this is not my decision. So, I thank Iris for her amazing offer, and tell her that I will ask Jake how he feels about it and get back to her soon.

Jake and I have a chat that evening about the possibility of him living with Iris, and I am pleasantly surprised that he thinks it's a great idea.

He says, "Absolutely, yes."

He doesn't mind that he'll have to ride the bus for thirty minutes to get to school each day, or that he won't be living among students his own age. For Jake, this arrangement sounds like a plan that could work really well.

So, the following day I speak again with Iris and it is settled. Jake will move in with her and her little dog, Brandy. I honestly believe that this is a gift from the universe and breathe a huge sigh of relief knowing that Jake will not return to residence, a place that was filled with such negative experiences. That is a chapter that we can say good-bye to. He will now reside with the kindest, sweetest and most nurturing person I could imagine. It should feel closest to living at home, and I know it will be an uplifting and warm environment for Jake. It takes me back to the day Jake learned that he got his summer job position; that knowing, settling feeling that when you work hard you are rewarded with goodness. And Jake is being rewarded with goodness once again. I have always been a believer that when one puts in a good effort, with good intentions, then good comes back in return. Here is more proof.

~~~~~~

Mid-June and my gardens are done, the property looks ready; I can relax. I am still having some very emotional times. Barb and her family are never far from my mind. I know this part of grieving is normal. I have visited grief many times in my life before this. I know the pain of losing a sibling. It felt like my right arm was removed and my heart was left in pieces. I think about that when I think of Barb's sisters. You never fully recover, regardless of how much time passes. You learn to eventually move on with your life, sometimes with a little more ease, with each passing day. This is the journey of loss now for Barb's sisters. I think about Iris, and I do not know her pain, or the immense grief in the loss of her child. I can't even begin to imagine it. My heart breaks for her. I feel helpless and wish I could erase the pain for all of them.

~~~~~~

Years before the loss of my brother, my family and I experienced two other significant family losses; the kind of devastation that one reads about in the newspaper, but never imagines will ever occur in their own nucleus. The first I have no memory of in terms of the actual event, but I remember it as a frequent serious discussion in my family home. My mother's youngest sister, Isabel, married as a child bride, and just beyond her twentieth birthday had given birth to four children. These children, my cousins, were close in age to me and my brothers, and we grew up and spent much time together. Their father, my uncle Earl, barely an adult himself, was shot and killed following a night of excessive alcohol consumption, male testosterone, and a heated argument over a card game. The actual truth about his death was kept quiet, and I was never privy to the details until I was well into my forties. I had always been told that he was shot accidentally by his good friend. The final outcome was a charge of manslaughter and a two-year prison sentence. This outcome appeared to be acceptable for everyone, although I was never sure about my parents' true feelings in this matter.

My widowed aunt was left a single mom, and as a result needed to be close to her own mother and her siblings, in order to have the kind of strength and support needed to work and raise four young children. As a result, they spent a great deal of time with us, and my cousins felt like an extension of my own siblings. We were very close, sharing many play-dates, birthday parties, and holidays. Susan and Debbie were the two eldest girls, and John and Robbie their two younger brothers. I was closest to Debbie and John in both age and common interests, most especially in our teen years. But there were moments, with all of my cousins that will always remain special for me.

My aunt had an on-again-off-again boyfriend, named Ken. He was handsome and fun, to me a seeming Knight in shining armour, who arrived with an exuberance of joy, and swept us all off of our feet. Ken owned a motor boat, and he would indulge us children in days at the beach in his vessel. As a child, I had a recurring dream I was in the driver's seat of a car cruising along the highway. Flying across the water, in Ken's boat, the wind in my face, was the closest to that feeling of freedom my dream represented. It was magical.

I never quite understood, in my younger years, why my aunt had never married Ken. In my innocent and naïve young mind, he seemed like the kind of man who would give her a happily-ever-after life. But it was not to be, and as time passed, she and Ken parted ways.

My aunt eventually met another man and began to date more seriously. At this time, I was a teenager and was busy with my friends and my cousins, spending less time with adult relatives. I never met the man she dated, nor do I remember his name. What I do recall is the story of their relationship. After a few months of dating, her boyfriend informed my aunt that he was moving to the east coast of Canada. He invited her to move with him. Aunt Isabel declined. But this man continued to pursue her, from a distance, calling her on the phone and sending letters, begging her to join him. Eventually, she relented and agreed. Her eldest daughter, Susan was now married, Debbie was close enough to eighteen to make the decision not to move, and so Isabel packed up her two sons, John and Robbie and uprooted them to New Brunswick to live with her and her boyfriend. It was sad to see them leave, but we all wished them well.

I don't remember how long after the move we received the shocking and gut-wrenching news, but I will never forget where I was when I heard it. I was doing a shift at my part time job, at the local dry cleaners, when my eldest brother walked through the door. My parents had sent him to tell me to come home straight after work. I sensed something was terribly wrong and I begged him to tell me before he left.

My beloved, fun and crazy aunt, whom I adored, my cousin's beautiful mother had been killed, stabbed to death by her boyfriend. I was in shock. I was stunned with sadness, for myself, my immediate family, and my cousins. The news struck a chord like no other; it left me feeling scared and incredibly vulnerable. All of those seemingly sensationalized stories we watched on the news and read in the paper now proved to be true. This sort of thing really could happen to anyone. I was too young to remember my uncle's death, but now with the loss of my aunt, the reality of having not one, but two family members murdered was more than my young brain could process and makes sense of.

Death can bring people closer together or it can move them apart. Debbie, John and I, nearest in age, drew together in our grief. Debbie openly shared her raw and painful feelings over the loss of her mother. Susan, now pregnant with her first child took comfort in the arms of her husband. By default, Debbie took on the matriarchal role of caring for her brothers, a role she would continue to play well into their adulthood. John would often speak to me about the murder of his mother. He and Robbie were at home when it occurred. They were asleep in their beds, and then were suddenly awakened by the volatile argument and subsequent violence in the room next to theirs. The sound dissipated, and the boys eventually left the safety of their bedroom, only to find their mother lying in a pool of blood on the floor. Their lives were forever changed, and the post-traumatic stress left a calamitous imprint in their souls.

The truth could not be kept from me this time. The police report read that my aunt had been stabbed seven times with a butcher knife. The couple had been out with friends to celebrate a birthday and they had been drinking. Later, at home, an argument began, and Isabel had threatened to leave the relationship. Her enraged lover attacked and killed her. He was initially charged with second degree murder, but later accepted a plea bargain for manslaughter. He was given a far too light sentence of five years in prison; that final blow of injustice was too much for my family to bear. Two lives lost, too lenient a penance. We all struggled to find peace and closure.

As the years passed we didn't remain super close. Adulthood carried us to different cities and many varied lifestyles, but we still kept in touch. Eventually Debbie moved to a town close to where I now live, and we have remained closest of all of my cousins. We don't see each other often but she still keeps me abreast of her siblings' lives. Regardless, I always feel that tight family bond and carry a special place in my heart for the memories my cousins and I made growing up.

It is Debbie who calls me early this Sunday morning. Unless there was a family event being planned, we generally did much of our communicating via Facebook. So, when I see her name and phone number light up on the screen, I immediately sense it is bad news.

I answer the phone saying, "Debbie, I hope this isn't bad news."

I could hear that she was upset, and through her tears I hear her reply, "John was found dead in his apartment last night."

"Nooooo!" I am stunned and wail like a baby upon hearing this news. It is just more than I think I can bear, and it's crushing.

My cousin John, in his early fifties had been suffering with Chronic Obstructive Pulmonary Disease, unbeknownst to us, and had died of complications, alone in his home. This news couldn't be possible! John was always the light, always the jokester, always seemingly full of life. How could he be gone, too?

Enough is enough. Although I feel a sense of self-pity for my own loss, this blow to my cousins just seems so incredibly unfair to a family that has already had more loss than they deserve. I feel immense anguish and helplessness for my three remaining cousins. This added loss is just more horrible news which I cannot erase, or make better, in any way.

My cousin's service is not to be held for several more weeks. I want and need some kind of closure, a reality check. My mind is still in a state of disbelief. I keep in touch with some of the family members online, checking in, but not able to offer much comfort. I want to make the pain stop and make it all better for everyone, but of course I can't. Grief is so individual, and I have always had a deep respect in allowing it to unfold as it needs to, giving space, time, and understanding to those it touches. It aches, it screams, it comes in waves, and it transforms us into something unrecognizable at times; it's a painful part of living, and we never really want to get to a place where we expect the worst to be the norm. Death doesn't come with an invitation, and we are never really prepared for it.

~~~~~~

I am grateful at this time that Jake is living in the city and has the support of his brother. Even so, I would cast all of my emotional pain aside and focus on Jake, if I needed to. I am thankful that I can break from it to take time to grieve and to be a little kinder with myself. Jake is also happier to be with his brother and be able to live a little more independently at this time. I know that he's now doing fine. I learned that, initially, Jake took to binge watching YouTube videos on his laptop, each night after work and on weekends. Nick told me that he gave Jake a couple of weeks to settle in, and then he took it upon himself to encourage his brother to spend his down time, after work and on weekends, with some healthier activities, ones that would be more fulfilling and productive than online interactive gaming and binge-watching endless hours of YouTube videos and Anime. The beautiful part in all of this is that Jake respects and listens to Nick, and apparently is now giving his full effort to engaging in change.

I learn that Jake is helping with cooking, cleaning, and doing laundry, and that he has started sketching and programming for fun. He is working out with Nick and the two of them are playing some tennis at a local club. Jake tells me that he's starting to feel a lot of self-pride and is enjoying the process of applying himself and his talents towards some of his personal interests.

I remember our earlier conversation when Jake admitted that

he'd just rather play instead of needing to always work. After several weeks at his summer work, I ask Jake, "How do you feel now about participating in such a grown-up lifestyle, getting up and going to work five days a week?"

"It's great and actually better. When I go to work, I get to leave and go home at the end of the day, and my free time is mine to do whatever I want. But when I attend school, I have classes and schoolwork all day long, and then I leave school and still have more work to do. It feels like there's never any time to play," he answers.

Now, I completely understand why he finds school such a challenge, and why in parts of first and second year of university he relinquished all school responsibility and fell into the world of online gaming. It really was just too overwhelming, and there was no balance between work and play. He had no time to re-charge, and all of his energy was being sucked away by the demanding, yet prosaic responsibilities of school. I see even more now, that effective time management is going to be essential for Jake to be able to handle school again in the fall. He will have to learn to find some balance between work and play and understand that it's not always a 50/50 situation. I feel confident that working a 9-5 schedule and hanging out with and watching Nick is exactly where he needs to be right now. He is learning how to manage his time in a healthy way. It doesn't take away the fact that school may still be a grind, but it may encourage Jake to make the most of what little free time he will get. It will be important to make smarter decisions when he does get time to refresh.

Chapter 33

It's Father's Day, and Brian heads into the city to spend the afternoon and evening hanging with Nick and Jake. He tells me later that they snooped through the shops in Nick's neighbourhood and then enjoyed a dinner together. I love it when the guys spend time together and wish there were more of those moments. Brian spent so much of Nick and Jake's childhood working hard and travelling with his career that he missed out on many occasions to bond more closely with them. They all get along, that's not an issue, but their relationship is a little more superficial. When there are emotional issues to talk about, Nick and Jake generally still come to me to discuss them. Dad is the guy who is handy and can fix anything around the house that's broken; this is where he excels with problem solving. He's very attuned with crafting up innovative ideas for building and has worked hard over the years to create our beautiful home, with his hands and his many tools. Brian also loves to cook and is a fabulous chef in the kitchen. Both Nick and Jake have learned to never be afraid to try their own hand at food prep, and Nick has gained a love for creating many of his own tasty feasts. The great thing is that although Brian doesn't often initiate spending time with our sons, he never refuses to when it's suggested by them or me. We still spend a great deal of family time as a group. And throughout the spring and summer we see the guys for more special holidays, dinners in the city, and extended family gatherings.

With Jake now finding a good rhythm between work and play and living the city life with Nick, I am able to finally relax and focus more on work, fitness, friendships, and my relationship with Brian. I continue to keep pace with my fitness buddy and good friend Cindy, participating in exercise classes three mornings a week and also doing our daily power walk. We use this time to talk out whatever is bothering us and to share the mini-victories in our lives, to bounce ideas off of each other and to laugh about life, as much as we can. We know that no family is perfect and there are always kinks to work out, but we have a good idea what it takes to keep the pulse of our families flowing in a healthy direction. Cindy has daughters and one of them is in university, so she understands the grind and the anxieties that come with keeping our kids motivated. At least a couple times a week I receive a text from Jake describing with great excitement tidbits about what projects he's working on at his summer job. It is during my walks with Cindy that I share these and we both have a good giggle. It's all technology talk and it is way beyond our comprehension but sounds very impressive. And we know that Jake is thoroughly engaged and captivated by it, so it serves two purposes. It entertains us, and it also gives us a sense that Jake has settled in, is happy, and is thriving. Jake knows we enjoy it, knows we get a laugh, and so he keeps them coming. Since Cindy has been along for the ride, as one of my confidants through Jake's crisis, she is invested in hearing about his successes almost as much as I am. I am blessed to have that kind of reinforcement.

The last month has been a bit of a reprieve for me in terms of Jake's care and supervision, but it certainly hasn't been a time of ease for me, personally. There's no escaping whatever other stresses life throws at us, even while we're dealing with a big issue. While I am aware of all that is needed for me to continue to monitor Jake's progress, I also understand my need for self-care. I count my blessings that Jake is in a safe place with his brother and know that there are still months and years ahead of me supporting Jake through the remainder of his university career.

I take this time to exhale just a little bit. For now.

Chapter 34

August comes, and our family participates in two annual events. The Rogers Cup Tennis Masters Series comes to Toronto, and this year it will be Nick and I who give our time to volunteer at the event for ten days. Some years Jake has also joined us, but he is unable to take off any time from work. Brian doesn't volunteer but helps with driving, as needed, and he always attends a match or two. The second event is Barb's annual barbecue, and even though she is no longer with us, everyone who participates agrees that we will continue the legacy every summer now in her honour. Both events are fun, one much more meaningful and heartfelt than the other. It's so nice that everyone can gather together and share their favourite memories of Barb. These friendships have spanned many years and we're all happy that we will continue to nurture them. August also brings the celebration of Brian's mom's birthday, and this year she turns 101 years old. She is still doing amazingly well, still living on her own and in good health. It is rare to know someone at this ripe age, let alone be related to them. While last year we hosted a large 100th birthday party for her, this year it is lower key and just the five of us go out for a lovely dinner to celebrate. She enjoys being with her family and adores her grandsons. At her age we don't want to worry her, so she isn't aware of the circumstances we've dealt with over the past several months with Jake. She is very happy just to see everyone's smiling, healthy faces. For Brian, Nick, Jake and I, it is also a celebration of a successful summer, as we come down to the last month before Jake returns to school.

Jake has had an amazing experience in his summer job. He has learned much and gotten a sense of what his world will look like after he graduates and begins to embark on a full time-career. The summer break is winding down, and the company Jake works for hosts a staff party for all of its employees. Jake organizes carpooling with a co-worker, so he can attend. He tells me all about it the next time we speak. He is super-excited to tell me how well-organized the event was and how much fun he had. He's feeling quite pleased with himself for all that he's accomplished. He is especially excited that his boss took him aside at the party to express how happy he has been with Jake's work, and to make the offer to have Jake back at the company the following spring. Hearing this news brings a smile to my face; I'm happy for my son. Although I am not surprised at his work ethic and his ability to get along well with co-workers, it is still nice to know that someone else recognizes and appreciates those qualities in Jake. The fact that he has a summer job to walk into next year is a testament to the hard work he has done, both personally and professionally these past many months. I am grateful to the company for giving Jake a chance, and for grooming him, somewhat, for his future in the technology field.

Jake has been as diligent as possible about taking his herbal remedies, eating right, and exercising while living with his brother. He has established some excellent habits by spending his down time in healthy activities. He has come to realize that he is now able to play a little video-gaming on a console for short periods of time. He doesn't need to engage in multi-player interactive games that seem to go on endlessly. These games drain his time and energy and create the risk of getting sucked into a vortex of never-ending battle. But a brief game or two of a single-player game provides enough entertainment to satisfy his need for amusement. And he's added a list of many other pastimes that bring him personal satisfaction and gratification. Jake has returned to art and creative writing. He's also learned to schedule himself and take on the responsibility of attending to a job. He has done no counselling sessions with a professional since April, but he had Nick to talk through any of his concerns and frustrations. He has registered for his second-year courses, on time, and feels confident about returning to start second year in his Software Engineering program, sans the co-op portion.

At this time last year Jake realized he had lost the opportunity to participate further in the co-op program, creating much of his anxiety about starting second year. Now he's put himself in a scenario very similar to co-op, by securing another summer with this amazing technology company. He will re-enter university with four months of industry hands-on coding and programming experience, which will enhance his confidence. And he has a wonderful home to move into with someone he knows well and adores, who has offered him creature comforts similar to his family home. It is an exciting time for him and for me. There is much to look forward to and every reason to believe that Jake can succeed. There is also an overriding feeling that we're not out of the woods, so to speak, just yet. School is tough, and Jake's program is quite challenging; the workload can be heavy at times, and there will be less time for activities that Jake enjoys. Nick will not be present each day and Jake will be navigating his way across town on transit; school is no longer walking distance. Jake hasn't established a social network at school or in Guelph, and I will not be walking him to classes to get him started this time. For now, focusing on feeling confident that Jake has what it takes to move forward and succeed will overshadow any misgivings I may have. I will assume all is well while I continue to keep my eyes and ears open for the possibility that I am needed again to intervene.

~~~~~~

Before Jake returns to school, we have an afternoon alone on our front porch. It's a beautiful day, and we are reveling in the late summer heat, knowing that soon the days will begin to cool as fall awaits us just around the corner. We're enjoying a cold beverage and I feel close to Jake; a bond between us has grown as a result of his willingness to come forward months ago and share vulnerability and courage. I feel a pull to broach a delicate subject that has sat with me in discomfort for quite some time. I want to know and yet I am afraid of the answer. My need for clarity outweighs my fear, and I take the risk.

I say to Jake, "Do you recall that evening that I came to visit you in your previous school residence and there was that horrible odour coming from your room?"

"Yes," he replies.

"You told me that it was your dirty recycle containers that smelled, but it seemed far worse a stench to me than that."

"Yes," he says.

"What was it, really?" I ask.

I am floored by his formidable and sad answer.

"That was the smell of me dying, mom."

These are words that no parent ever wants to hear, and they leave my soul feeling utterly fractured. If it was never clear to me before just how deep the struggle was for Jake during that first semester of year two, it is now markedly evident. Hearing those words is a blistering slap of reality for me, and I now fully recognize that we dodged a fast-moving bullet.

Jake is telling me that he was literally dying; he'd given up, he was checking out. A deep, despondent, gut-wrenching awareness has shifted within me and I am speechless. Suddenly the tears come forth in one giant rush, and I reach out and grab Jake, folding him into my arms, sharing my immense anguish and intense love for him. If there was ever any doubt that his life was in need of saving just a few short months ago, it is certainly evident now, and the thoughts of what could have been overwhelm me like a tsunami. I am struck by a feeling of desolation and horror at what might have been. I have a momentary flash of the time that Jake was a baby and not thriving, at times seeming so fragile. And then I see Jake lying in bed, as a teenager, so ill and lifeless. We have witnessed Jake's near-departure before and to know it came to this point again is agonizing. The realization that Jake is still here and is very alive, healthier and stronger eventually returns to me, and there are no words powerful enough to describe my gratitude in having this second chance with my son.

Chapter 35

In early September, after we have marked my birthday with a celebratory dinner and the Labour Day holiday Monday arrives, I drive to Toronto and help Jake pack up his belongings at Nick's apartment. Then we carry on to Guelph to move him officially into his next temporary home. In the past twelve months Jake has lived in our family home, in two different school residences, and in his brother's apartment; all this moving requires much flexibility and adaptability which is not easy for someone with an anxiety disorder. It will be nice for him to be settled finally into one place for the next two semesters.

We are greeted with a warm and inviting welcome by Iris and her little dog, and then we begin the process of moving Jake in. He has been given much of the large basement for his dwelling and has a bedroom, sitting area, and a two-piece bathroom. It's a walk-out so has really good lighting; it will be perfect for Jake's needs and a far cry from the tiny space he would have had in a school dorm room. Iris and Jake will have meals together upstairs. I feel immediately that Jake will be nurtured and possibly spoiled, so there are no concerns about Jake's basic needs being met. And although I do not expect Iris to be responsible for Jake's well-being, I am certain that if she were to sense that something wasn't quite right with Jake, she would either inquire with him or speak with me, or both. I do know that if Jake were to fall back into an old pattern, staying up all night playing online video games and not attending school, Iris would go looking for him. There is definitely reassurance for me in that, and I am appreciative.

Back home, Brian and I continue in the empty nest phase, more focused on our relationship, with the understanding that this time for just us could be temporary. We're feeling more hopeful this time that Jake will have more success under the periodic influence of his brother and the confidence he's gained in his summer job experience. We would, of course welcome him back home if that was needed, but Brian and I understand that it's not what Jake wants. His anxiety seems less acute than this time last year. Jake seems better able to cope.

Upon my continued prodding, Brian has recently had a physical check-up with our family physician and followed it up with some usual tests. During a routine colonoscopy the specialist found a problem that requires immediate medical attention. After years of Brian suffering through many bouts of Diverticulitis, a section of his bowel has developed scar tissue that has now created a significant narrowing. If left unattended, it will eventually create a blockage at this site. We're happy that it's been discovered early and can be remedied with an operation. I have worried about Brian's health for some time now, as typical of many men, he ignores signs and signals when he doesn't feel 100%, and rarely seeks the counsel of his doctor. I am relieved that my concerns have finally been addressed, but I also understand the magnitude of an operation of this kind.

Just two weeks after Jake starts school Brian enters the hospital for surgery, in Toronto, to remove about twelve inches of his large intestine. It's a serious and major operation that takes a few hours to complete. I wait at the hospital to hear word from the surgeon, and when I do I am relieved to hear everything went well. For some reason, the recovery room nurses don't communicate with me, and it is several more hours before I am able to see Brian, post-surgery. That time is far more stressful than awaiting word about the outcome of his surgery. It is one thing to be told that your husband is fine, but for some reason my brain needs my eyes to witness him in person and I don't relax until I am finally by his bedside and know that he's okay. He's hooked up to lots of wires and machines, and he is resting. The next twenty-four hours are important, as infection is a possibility. I return home to get a good night's sleep.

The following day I receive great news about Brian, and recovery should go smoothly from here on. I have collected both Nick and Jake and they visit him at the hospital with me. I have put in a lot of mileage today, and so Jake and I decide to spend the night in Toronto at Nick's place.

The following evening, after another visit with Brian, who is resting well with pain meds, Jake and I drive back to Guelph. He looks good; he tells me that school is going well and that he is very happy living with Iris. I start feeling the stress of Brian's surgery and all the driving in the last few days and realize that I'm physically and emotionally exhausted. I ask Jake if he would mind if I spend the night in Guelph. He's good with this. Iris has invited me to stay for dinner, and when we arrive back at her home, I request an overnight stay. She is more than gracious.

The following morning Jake goes back to school and I have a lovely breakfast and visit with Iris before driving back to the city to see Brian. When I arrive at the hospital Brian is up and dressed and packed up ready to go home. He has been given the green light by the doctor this morning and he is being discharged. He's still quite weak and heavily-medicated, but it is a relief to know that he is well enough to come home. On the way, we stop at the pharmacy to pick up more pain medication, and then we are on our way home, finally. I have been away from the house for two days and Brian has been away for three, and both of us are happy to be able to put hospitals and doctors behind us for a while. I can now continue Brian's care in the comfort of our home.

We walk in via the back door of our house and into our kitchen. It feels so good to be home. But then I suddenly hear a strange noise, and ask, "What's that sound?"

It appears as though someone may be in our house. Fear creeps in. I continue walking through the kitchen and arrive at the entrance to our living room and am hit with a horror!

~~~~~~

It is raining inside our home, a deluge of water streaming down. Our living room ceiling is bleeding saturated and glutinous clumps of drywall paste and puddles of water onto our wood floors and our carpet. I feel my pulse quicken in panic. Something has burst or broken, and our home is flooding, and I need to stop it now!

I immediately sprint up a flight of stairs to our second floor and follow the sounds of gurgling water, in order to find the source. Inside our en suite bathroom the brass pipe on the outside of our claw foot tub has burst, and there's a steady flow of water discharging onto the marble flooring. I swiftly turn off the valve attached to the pipe to put a stop to any further damage. I am not left feeling any sense of relief, seeing the magnitude of the situation ahead of us. I hear Brian on his way up the stairs; he is jacked up on pain meds and all he wants to do is lie down on our bed. In his weakened condition, he can't offer to help much. As the man of the house, he will feel a need to do something, but as a sick patient he will have to submit to the rest that his body needs. I run to help him up the rest of the stairs and into bed, where the area is still dry. I turn and stand amid the chaos. The house is in a dismal state and I realize that I need back up. I need immediate and strong assistance to handle this mess. I tell Brian not to worry and that I will deal with things; he just needs to stay put.

I call the best person I know for handling a crisis, my good friend Cindy. Thankfully, she is home and is available to come and help. I grab buckets and towels and try to at least reduce some of the flood damage, but it is like sticking a small bandage on a broken bone. The amount of water pouring forth and the damage it is creating is overwhelming. When I call our insurance company on the phone, I am greeted with a voice that brings instant comfort. He tells me that someone will come immediately to assess the damage and start a claim. He is kind, soft-spoken, exactly what I need at this moment.

Cindy arrives and takes over, without requiring any instructions, and that's a relief, as I just don't know where to begin. My brain is focused on catering to Brian's needs, while I continue to provide information to the man on the other end of the phone. Cindy searches and finds more buckets, and then she calls her husband to come and help also.

While I am still on the phone, I am suddenly hit on the head with something wet, and I scream. Pieces of the ceiling are falling in great clumps now, and the insurance rep soon realizes how serious the situation is. Everything is moving very quickly. Cindy's husband arrives with more helpers, and people are running around cleaning up water and moving furniture away to safety. I feel like I am in a daze, a nightmarish scene playing out all around me.

Very soon the restoration representative arrives at the house and brings with him a much-needed soft and kind energy. Eventually, with all of this amazing assistance around me now, I am able to focus on formulating a plan.

The restoration rep has explained that we will not be able to remain in our home and will need to arrange to evacuate as soon as possible. Hotel and food costs will be covered by insurance. I explain that due to the nature of Brian's surgery, I cannot feed him restaurant meals as it would be detrimental to his recovery. I am told to ask for a hotel room with a kitchenette so that I may still be able to cook, and the insurance company will pay the extra for us to have more space and amenities. In the meantime, Brian is still asleep upstairs, so I wake him to tell him that we will be moving to a hotel room. I am able to call and reserve us a suite with a local hotel. What feels like mere minutes has likely been a couple of hours, but I lost total track of time amid the turmoil. I have packed bags for Brian and I, and we express our gratitude to our friends, thank the restoration rep, who is now taking over our home, and then we are on our way to a nearby hotel. I am aware of the situation, and yet I feel like I am mindlessly going through the motions, and in a robotic state.

There are blessings in darkness, and if you look closely enough and are open to receiving them, they will certainly appear. This lesson has been made very clear to us throughout Jake's trials and tribulations. Jake's first illness led me into studying Iridology. While sick as a teenager Jake discovered that being in school has its benefits. Now monitoring Jake through university has allowed us I to spend more time communicating. My husband has a difficult time with sitting still, and I am very concerned about how much rest he'll actually get, post-surgery. Many people might think that recovering from surgery while living in a hotel would be just insane, but for us, this situation has its upsides. Although there are days of discomfort and Brian has much fatigue to deal with, over the next few weeks he does manage to remain stationary long enough to make a full and healthy recovery. Without the distractions of projects, he'd usually want to tackle at home, he has been forced to rest, and I am grateful.

The damage to our home exceeds $50,000 and will require a lengthy time for restoration. Although we have a kitchenette, it is really just a fridge and a microwave. Friends and neighbours very kindly prepare us lovely meals to heat up. The hotel provides a daily hot breakfast. When Brian is able to travel short distances, we take trips to Nick's apartment and use his kitchen to prepare more food to take back with us to the hotel. Once Brian begins to have more strength, several of our friends do their part in getting us out of the hotel suite and invite us to dinners and even movies. Cindy gets me out for daily hikes and fresh air. Girlfriends come by the hotel to have tea or coffee and visit with me. Somehow, we manage well, so far, in this crisis. I feel as though I have become practiced in handling surprise catastrophes during the past year, but not without the generosity and kindness of our wonderful circle of friends. There are not enough words for the gratitude I feel. The plan is to be back in our home in a very short time, but as we have learned in the past many months, plans can change, and flexibility and fortitude are required.

Chapter 36

In all the kerfuffle, we are temporarily-diverted from our concerns for Jake. Thankfully, he has Iris in his corner. By the end of September Brian feels strong enough to take a visit with me to Guelph, and we have dinner with both Iris and Jake. Our son looks happy, and he tells us that school is going well. He has made some new friends in his program and is doing a large group project in his computer design class. He is also enjoying his English elective. Iris has created a great living space for Jake in her basement, and so he has privacy when he needs it, and a large work space for doing homework assignments. Although I am dealing with Brian's recovery and making the best of our new living arrangements, I still make time to stay in touch with Jake via email and text. I notice that he responds with more promptness and regularity than first semester one year ago, and I take this as a good sign. It is a completely different experience to have healthier communication with Jake and one that is so welcome, especially now.

In early October Nick comes to visit and spends a weekend in Guelph with Jake. We join them on the Saturday evening and the two of them prepare a fantastic birthday dinner for Brian. And on the Thanksgiving weekend both Nick and Jake stay in a room at the hotel where we are now residing. We celebrate both Thanksgiving and Jake's birthday together. We say goodbye to the teen years, and hello to a new decade, as Jake is now twenty years old. He's two years into adulthood and seems to be maturing in leaps and bounds.

The flood restoration drags on well beyond projections, and it takes close supervision by Brian to keep it moving forward. The contractor and workers make many mistakes, resulting in delay after delay. It becomes quite taxing, and I worry about Brian's health, again. My business takes a back seat, and I see clients only if they are local and if they are willing for me to make a house call. I am so blessed for my clients' patience, understanding and flexibility, despite the inconvenience the flood has presented. I have many more hours now for writing, and so I shift my focus to that, while always keeping one eye on Jake, ready and available, as needed.

As the mid-term period at school unfolds, Jake mentions that the assignment deadlines and his mid-term tests are fast approaching. At this point I am assuming that he is managing well and am hoping that he can handle this next expectation.

As more time passes I start to hear less and less from Jake through text and email, and that triggers worrisome memories, and my mind starts to go to places that I really don't welcome visiting. At times, during my writing process, I find myself feeling some of the same emotions I had experienced at the time of those terrifying events. I get panicked and uneasy, and I sometimes have to check in with Jake just for some momentary reassurance that he's fine. Today is one of those days, so I send Jake a text that reads:

You haven't been sharing as much as you normally do, and that sends little alarm bells off inside of me. It's especially hard when I am writing about your past. You okay? xo

Jake replies immediately:

Yeah, I'm just kind of stressed with the last of my projects and midterm coming up Friday. I met with my Special Needs Advisor today, told her how I was doing and what I was doing to handle things. She thought I was doing a fantastic job, but also told me not to beat myself up over feeling drained during my down time and not wanting to do my hobbies due to such fatigue. I've been upset with myself because I've been writing, drawing, and programming for myself lately, and just want to relax and watch videos or something, shut down my brain for a bit. I then attribute that to being bad, based on my time in university before and my time with Nick, where I had to do productive things after work every day. If I didn't and watched a couple videos (even just one video), he would get on my case, worrying about how I may be slipping back into spiraling downwards. It's put a lot of extra stress on my head, and my advisor told me that sometimes it's alright to just power down, because you need it. I really need to rest, my head is tingling and buzzing and won't stop, it's driving me up the wall. But I just have to get through the last couple of questions of this assignment, write the midterm, and work on the new assignment in data structures that'll come out tomorrow, build the skeleton for my software design project, start thinking about my English essay that'll be coming up soon, do the new micro computing assignment, read two novels - It's endless, it really is. I just want to play a game or watch something mindless. I want to be me, do the things I want to do, but I don't have the time. I can't write, except on the bus, but only if I can get my mind off everything else. I can't play video games because you'll get upset and I don't want to worry you. I can't draw because that requires multiple HOURS of free time. I don't want to do programming for myself, because I'm doing that in Python, and I already have to balance working in Java, learning assembler and relearning C. The last thing I need is another programming language to muddle my thoughts. Thank God I have music to listen to, because it feels like the last damn freedom I have. I feel shackled, to be honest. I've felt shackled since gaming was taken away from me. Not because of an addiction to games, but it's like telling a kid they can no longer play their favourite sport. It's a pastime I really REALY enjoy, and I can't partake. I know why, I understand the dangers and that I don't have the time, but do you have any idea how stressful it is to think that if I do one of the things I enjoy most, my family will lose their shit on me? You'll worry and start asking me incessantly if the games are ruining my life, because of how things went before, and Nick will just be disappointed, and I'm sure dad has an opinion he doesn't voice to me about it.

Jake's reply is a clear glimpse into his world and an eye opener that I can really appreciate. I respond with:

I can really feel your frustration. This is a very busy part of school and requires a lot of your time and focus. I know it's hard not to be able to do stuff you enjoy. I have crunch times like that in my business and feel resentful that I can't play. I barrel on through and then take a bigger break. You'll have that in December and can blow off steam and rest your brain while snowboarding on the slopes. What can I do to help in the meantime?

He replies:

There's nothing you can do, sadly. I'm on my own for this. I can't just hand you my work and say, "Good luck." I'm already getting the help I need from others, discussing the problems and learning. I'm absorbing information from the lectures just fine, it's tough work, and it'll stay tough. Please keep checking in on me though, it's a nice reminder that you care.

This kind of clarity really helps us both. I know how much to step in and offer, and I am also reassured that Jake has a lot of help at the school level. I suggest that my husband and I visit him on campus soon, and Jake agrees that this would be helpful.

~~~~~~

My husband and I visit Jake a couple days later and have brunch with him at school. We want to show our support and see, in person, how Jake is doing. A lot can be hidden in a text message, as I've come to learn. I take along an extra herbal remedy for Jake to help take the edge off of his stress. He looks and smells good; he's not losing weight; his eyes are clear and so is his skin. He seems to be managing well in spite of the stress. Perhaps our visit will help to ground him and keep him going through the rest of midterms. We have an upbeat conversation over brunch, before Jake has to head to his next lecture. We embrace, a big hug, some words of reassurance that he's going to get through this phase just fine, and then we're on our way.

I stay in touch with him daily through the weekend. On the Monday I send the following text:

Good morning. How are you feeling about facing another school week? It's okay if you're not feeling great about it. You don't always have to report only good stories.

I would prefer to be able to say this over the phone, and against my better judgement send it via text. It's early in the morning and I don't want to disturb him with a phone call if he's rushing to get to class. I also want Jake to know that he doesn't have to hide from me when he's feeling frustrated or stressed. I am trying to be supportive in any way possible, unsure of just how much I need to give, and how much I need to just let go and trust; this is the balancing act I am still working through.

Jake replies with the following text:

To be honest, you asking me repeatedly is making me feel a bit pressured. I get that you're worried about me but I'm okay. It seems like you think I'm in a really bad place right now.

And as I suspected might be the case, my text is misunderstood. That's the problem with sending any communication that has emotional content via email or text. It doesn't always convey what you want it to. The receiver gets to decide how the message is supposed to come across, based on their feelings at the time. Unfortunately, he has read it with a very different tone than I had implied. So, I reply:

Actually, I'm trying to convey that I am not worried about you. When things are going well you share a lot with me and I love hearing from you. And then when things are not so upbeat you tend to go quiet and I miss hearing from you. What I was trying to say is that any news from you, good or not so good, is welcome. I don't want you to think you can't share because you think it will upset me or worry me. I asked you on Friday, over brunch, if you thought you had what it takes to get through this semester, and you looked me in the eyes and said, "Yes." And I believe you. You also told me in a text, to continue to check in because it's good for you to know that I care. I want to do only what is best for you, and adding pressure is not my goal. So, sorry, Sweetie that it came across in that manner.

Jake sends a text back immediately:

Thanks mom. I'm feeling confused by micro computing, but after today, after I get some help from Tyler (he understands it well), I'll be in the clear. I'm looking forward to working on software design tomorrow. Also, I got my English midterm back. I got 75.5%.

I never want to harp on or impose expectations about grades, and I also am careful about making too much out of a good grade, as it can create too much pressure for a consistently high performance. So, although I want to say "Hooray" to his English mark, I also don't want to give the impression that it's the most important thing he could share with me. I also want to have Jake see that I am confident that he is handling things well, but again, don't want to gush over it and add pressure that he has to always be on top of his game. The goal is not to strive for perfection, but for him to simply do the best that he can. So, I simply text:

Thanks for sharing.

And then we both get on with our day. He knows where I'm at, and that I trust him, and I am happy that he's communicating again. I breathe a sigh of relief, not because Jake is fine, but because I was able to convey a loving message without coming across as some kind of manic, hovering mom, and I am still able to keep our line of communication open. We're two adults conversing, and although one of us is the parent and one of us is the adult child, there's a passage that needs to be reached, so that we can continue to respect each other's boundaries, and progress in our relationship.

Sometimes I feel I am walking on a tightrope, trying to maintain a balance, fearing that just one misinterpreted statement will have either of my sons metaphorically pushing me right off the rope, with no hope of getting back up. I parent from a very conscientious place, wary that I can inadvertently find myself in this precarious position. I am well aware of communication breakdowns and know that something well-meaning can be easily misconstrued. For the most part, my sons are now in control of how much I get to be a part of their lives. This shift is a huge part of that transition between parenting one's child and parenting one's adult child.

We as parents no longer fit them into our lives; they now decide when and how we fit into theirs. Although we may want a close and loving relationship, I am always aware that each person's definition of family closeness can vary in small and large ways. Yes, I want to be included in their lives, but I also understand that there are many areas that are none of my business. This balancing act is a necessary process to work through, to instill confidence in our adult children, and to let them know that we believe they can manage their lives well, while also conveying an interest in who they are and how they're conducting their lives. I know that Jake needs us to support him through his time at university, but he doesn't have to choose to accept this, and when he's irritated and frustrated by a heavy workload, he can make some regrettable decisions. We've been witness to this unpredictable time already, and so there's a certain degree of white-knuckling through it all, without ever feeling one hundred percent secure that it will be smooth sailing from here on in. There's no guarantee that he won't isolate himself from us if he feels too much pressure or misconstrue our good intentions. The risk of being misconstrued is never a bad thing; it keeps me in line as a parent and reminds me never to take our relationship for granted.

The second part of this balancing act is knowing which person I am meeting when I make contact with my maturing sons. While in their presence, talking with them on the phone, or receiving an email or text, there are times I need to decipher if this is the person partnering with me, adult to adult, or if this is the still developing quasi-adult needing maternal intervention and care. And I have to know when to move in and offer parental advice, or just to enjoy some meaningful time where we're both on equal footing. I do know this, for sure – if I get it wrong, both Nick and Jake are quick to jump in and ask me to back off. I hate getting it wrong. But I have always been open about having them check me when I am overstepping my boundaries. And I'm not above apologizing and working on doing better next time. We are in essence each other's teachers.

Chapter 37

    Jake continues to work hard through all of his mid-term projects and tests, and then his school routine eases off a bit as he moves through the second half of the semester. He seems to manage it well and stays in touch with me with some regularity. The flood restoration has had more setbacks, and it's difficult some days not to be frustrated. When I start to get into a funk about it, I try to take a moment and re-focus on all that I have to be grateful for, and then I am able to find my Zen again. There are people suffering with illness, those who are losing loved ones, folks who are living on the streets, and I can't complain. I have a roof over my head and hotel staff who treat me with warmth and dignity; I have my health and my wonderful family and friends. I also know that being a good role model under this pressure cooker of a situation can only be a benefit for Jake. Our children see our actions, and continue to learn from them, no matter whether they are children or adults. I still have that responsibility to shoulder, and it's important he knows the irritants of the situation as well as the tools I'm using to get through it in a healthy manner.

Jake and I have a discussion about how he's found better ways to manage school and the stressors that come with it. He tells me that after hitting rock bottom and then learning that he could not only survive a crisis, but that he could also rise above it, he now realizes that disasters are not the end of the world. He doesn't fear failure now, and he understands that if he loses momentum and gets behind or fails a credit again, it may be a long haul back, but he knows he can do it. He understands where to turn for help and he is grateful to have his family behind him, as well as all of the support systems that the University of Guelph has in place when he is feeling overwhelmed.

Jake also understands that if he's going to stay away from online gaming, he has to engage in activities that are fun, challenging and have a structured sense of purpose, in order to create the high level of stimulation that gaming provides. After many months of gaming the brain gets used to that high dopamine level, and replacing it requires an action-packed experience to duplicate the adrenaline rush to what is considered his brain's norm. Spending time enduring mundane tasks and times of stress are triggers that provoke the desire to escape to gaming. During their summer together, Nick suggested Jake come up with a list of high energy hobbies and sports he enjoys, and he taught him to organize these activities into what he terms "layers", prioritizing which are at the top and what's at the bottom of the list. The goal is to first choose from the top, whenever possible. Playing tennis, playing Ping-Pong, and graphic artwork all stimulate Jake and engage him in reasonable lengths of time. He has an order of importance for each activity, but if he's unable to participate, he knows what to choose as a good alternative. So, for example, if playing tennis is on top and there's no one available to play a game with, then next on his list may be to do some artwork. Jake also requires activities that can be used for relaxation and rest, that re-charge him following a stressful time. He now chooses reading and creative writing.

Jake tells me he feels he now is able to focus better since taking his supplements, eating healthy and getting regular exercise. I realize that his ADD is not something that will be cured; it is something that he will always have to manage. In terms of his level of attention deficit, Jake appears to be in moderate range. According to the research I've studied, so far, the later the symptoms appear, the less severe the ADD is. I recall when Jake was tested by the psychologist at age seven, it was noted at the end of the assessment that he had seen no signs of any behavioral disabilities. Jake's diagnosis came in adulthood. It's not that his mind doesn't still wander off and become easily distracted, or that his brain doesn't continue to spin constantly with thoughts while taking a remedy. But he has noticed that instead of getting way off track and taking longer to get back to the task at hand, he now finds it easier to re-focus much sooner than he did before. This improved focus is really helping him to get through school assignments with more ease. He continues to find it challenging, and schoolwork continues to be a chore, but he's keeping his eye on the prize, so to speak, and meeting his deadlines, as needed. And he has decided to continue his regimen of healthy eating and taking his remedies. I, too check in with Jake regularly, and will offer more help, as needed. For now, he seems to be coping well.

~~~~~~

Mid-November I spend a fabulous day with Nick. I have had to spend an enormous amount of time focused on Jake, one-on-one, and it's a treat to now have some of that private time with Nick. It's lovely that he can take some time away from work, mid-week. We head to a little town not far from the hotel, where Nick starts the day with a fresh haircut, and then we take a walk to a nearby art gallery, checking out the paintings and pottery by local artists. We then have a beautiful lunch at a heritage restaurant that was once the town's mill. We talk, we laugh, and we enjoy good food. Nick has to go online to check in with his work project later in the afternoon, so we return to the hotel. We have dinner with Brian in the evening and then I drive Nick back to the city, happy and thankful to have shared such a wonderful day with my eldest son. It's the kind of time that allows me to step away, momentarily, from all the chaos that prevails. Here we are, living in a hotel, restoration has barely begun in our home, my health business is on a bit of a hiatus, and Jake is still struggling through midterms. In the back of my mind there is always that little voice reminding me that I must always be ready in the moment when tougher times may strike.

Not long after our day together, I hear from Nick again. He tells me that he's decided to adopt a cat from the Toronto Humane Society. I am thrilled for him. He grew up in a home with pets and knows the joys of having a four-legged companion. I realize that it's a big step for him; having a pet is a huge responsibility and commitment. I have no concerns that he is not ready for this. He will embrace his obligations maturely, and that cat will be one lucky feline to be in his care. By the end of the day I learn that he has brought home a two-year-old female cat named Booker, and I feel so much joy for the two of them. I am glad that another animal has been saved from a shelter. No parental advice is needed here. I know my role is to just express my happiness.

Near the end of November, Brian and I visit Jake, and have dinner with him in his Guelph home. I notice that he's looking thin, he seems awkward around me, and he's a little shaky. Something feels off, and I ask him about it. He looks surprised at my inquiry and tells me he's fine. But he seems edgy and defensive. I start to wonder if he's really okay, or if he's distracted by too much Internet recreation. I know that school has been very demanding this semester, and he felt suffocated through midterm, and I suspect he's found some unhealthy responses to the stress. I know that he's nearing the finish line and there will be more projects and assignments with deadlines, followed by preparation for final exams. I make a mental note to check in and pay attention to my instinct. It hasn't let me down before, although I have not always listened to it. I'm learning.

I recall a conversation I had with Jake a few weeks ago, as we were sitting together and visiting. I mentioned to him that I still thank my lucky stars that he came clean with us last year and asked us for help. I also told him that I am still haunted by his shocking statement that the awful smell I had asked about in his dorm room was, in his words, the smell of him dying. Jake's response was that he would have never taken pills, hung or shot himself; those would not have been his choices. He had just checked out and stopped caring for himself, wasn't eating much, and was fading away. What a horribly long, slow, and painful way to meet death, I think to myself. Yet, there is a part of that statement that is reassuring. It's as though Jake is telling me that when he gave up and slowly withdrew, I had a chance of catching him before he disappeared into an abyss of no return. It's also a statement that leaves me feeling incredibly sad and scared. I am very aware that Jake has felt so incredibly low and depressed that he's broached the possibility of dying and given it this much thought. Jake's suffering has had an impact on me, that the sight of Jake losing even a few pounds and seeming even a little despondent sends my radar to high alert. But my fear is balanced by the many conversations expressing how much better Jake feels, and how much he now wants to live. I settle myself down, comforted by the knowing that Iris would notice Jake not eating and would most definitely inform me, and I allow myself to ease off the worry.

~~~~~~

In December Jake receives a lovely surprise and learns that his friend Eren, with whom he travelled through Tokyo last year, is in the United States visiting his girlfriend, and the two of them have made arrangements to visit Jake in Guelph for an overnight. This news lifts Jake's spirits, and gives him a fun break from the schoolwork he still has. I'm happy for all of them to have this opportunity to see each other in person. It's just what Jake needs right now; it's been all work and very little play for him these past few months.

Not long after this break, I receive a text from Jake, and it's like he's shouting from the rooftops:

I CAN PLAY GAMES AGAIN! I'M DONE ALL THE SEMESTER WORK! WOO OOO RELAXATION.

Do you still have to attend classes? I ask, and then quickly follow it with, BTW – congratulations!

Jake replies, Of course I still attend. It's just review, but that's still important. I missed only one lecture this semester, when we all rented out a room in the library to do an online quiz, and they wouldn't let me leave until we were all finished. I didn't mind it too much, since I still got the notes from that day, but it ruined my perfect track record this semester.

I text back, That's amazing Jake. You must feel so good about your success this semester. Bravo to you! Your first night free of homework! Does it feel liberatingly amazing?

I get a simple response: I'm playing games.

I know that I should be celebrating Jake's success, and I am happy for him. However, he still has to study for and write five final exams. And the thought of him playing video games, for many parents, might not be an issue. For Jake, it can get out of control pretty quickly when he's left unleashed. On the one hand, he's earned this down time and deserves to have some recreation and play. And perhaps he's matured enough this semester to be able to balance work and fun, and still stay focused on his academic goals. And I assume when he says that he's playing games, that he means short bursts of Game Cube, not the endless socially interactive games that he had become far too engrossed in and dependent on in the recent past.

I tell myself that there are only a few more days until classes finish, and then he will be here at the hotel, a somewhat more controlled environment. We can then talk about how best to set up a healthy schedule for studying and make a plan that works for both of us. I get that the idea of helping to set up a study schedule with a twenty-year-old might seem ridiculous and over the top. I never had to do such a thing with Nick, but then Nick is an entirely different person. He matured at a faster rate than Jake; he raced to be independent, and he didn't struggle with a mental health issue or learning disability. He also never asked for this kind of help. Jake has been slower to grow independent. He is also somewhat comfortable with having assistance and a strong support; he understands that he still needs to have accountability to help him with focus. He also wants to learn eventually to be able to handle his responsibilities on his own. Independence is the eventual goal. I can't place any judgement on the rate of personal growth between my two sons. They are two different people who are simply growing at a different rate. They each deal with day-to-day living in very unique ways and supporting their individual maturation requires a different approach from me. For now, I continue to do some micro-managing with Jake, but throughout this process I am constantly asking myself many questions:

How much is too much help?

Is this one of those times that I should let go?

Should I now allow Jake to stumble along, on his own again, learning through his mistakes?

Am I intervening to save him from himself?

Do I need to intervene to save him in this single moment?

Do I need to jump in to save his life?

That last one haunts me, especially when I look back a year ago and realize that Jake had begun to give up, he'd allowed the video gaming to control his life; he was barely eating, he was barely living. And there is always in the back of my mind the feeling that he could fall back so quickly down that very slippery slope again. I'm not sure that Jake is ready to shoulder full responsibility for his wellbeing just yet, nor am I. For now, I stop. I turn my worries off for the moment, and I breathe deeply. I have to believe that he'll be fine over the next few days.

Chapter 38

On the last day of Jake's classes, I have other commitments throughout the day, and then I have an event to attend that evening. I don't see Jake. Brian picks him up from school and drives him to the hotel. Nick joins him for the weekend.

The following day is a wonderful time spent together as a family. I begin to feel as though I can exhale and let my guard down, now that Jake is finished with classes and lectures. My favourite place to be is with my family; it matters not whether we are at home or in this hotel. We enjoy breakfast together and then we have a swim in the hotel pool. I start to sense, during breakfast that something isn't quite right. I notice Jake's behaviour seems a little shaky. But when I attempt to talk about it, Brian abruptly stops the conversation with a curt word, and I let it go. Perhaps I am being paranoid, maybe overly-cautious. It isn't worth it to me to delve any deeper and spoil a great day ahead of us.

In the afternoon we watch an entertaining Christmas special on the television in our suite. We then get dressed up and attend an annual open house party with friends in our neighbourhood. We return to the hotel later and play a couple of card games, talking, laughing and thoroughly enjoying each other's company. We are a family who loves to play together. Card games, board games, tennis matches, music concerts, and comedy festivals are all activities we have shared many times. We relish travel and have made so many fabulous memories visiting various parts of the world. And we are a family of foodies, so enjoying excellent meals that we either prepare at home or have prepared for us in a restaurant is also big on our list. We're loud, we talk a lot, we poke fun at each other, we tell jokes, and we laugh a ton. We all have individual interests and lives outside of family time, but when we gather as a group we truly embrace ourselves as one strong, bonded unit. Today is one of those kinds of days and it feels awesome.

The following day the glow of yesterday wanes, and I have this unsettled feeling in the pit of my stomach again. The sense that something isn't quite right is gnawing at me.

Mid-day, I knock on Jake's hotel door and when Nick answers I walk all the way down the length of the room to ask Jake something. And to my horror he is sitting at the desk with his laptop open and is playing that addictive multi-player online game! That game that nearly destroyed our lives; that game that took over all of his good sense, driving him into a deep, dark hole where he stopped truly living! I am furious at the sight of those mythical characters jumping off the screen, taunting me, and stirring up a sudden panic in me. I am instantly drawn in a flashback to a dangerous, darker time.

I am caught in a quandary. I want to address this and be done with it immediately. But I have no time for this; I am on my way out for the afternoon with Brian. But, I must take at least a few moments for this.

I ask Jake, "Why do you have this game loaded back on your computer?"

He looks so surprised. "I'm done my classes; I can play games now."

I look over at his brother's laptop and it's on his screen, as well. I realize that they have loaded the game, in preparation, and are now set up to play it together. I ask Nick, "Why are you encouraging this?"

He replies, "I'm trying to teach him."

I cut him off short and say, "You can't teach this."

I am enraged, and know that if I say anything more, I will create more hurt and regret than I want to. So, I walk out of the room. I need time to think this through and figure out how to handle it. By walking away, I realize that I am allowing the guys the afternoon to play their game. But that video game will most certainly be gone by evening, after my return. I will force the issue. I now see that this is a time when I will need to enforce my parental authority, regardless of the fact that Jake is a grown man. He cannot possibly risk losing all of the hard work he's accomplished, especially before he's written his exams. In a controlled environment, with Nick in the room, it will be fine. But he has the next two weeks, alone in his hotel room, unsupervised and with no accountability, and it would be so easy for him to fall prey to all of the enticements that this game has taunted him with before. I have visions of him up all night and sleeping all day, not answering the door when I knock to check in on him. I can feel him falling into that dark pit once more, and I am terrified.

I am also very annoyed with Brian. My gut instinct was correct, once again, and instead of being on the same page and supporting me, he undermined my authority as a parent, and didn't want me to question Jake. Consequently, we have our own discussion about this, in private, and I make it very clear that his inability to recognize that Jake is in trouble and needs our intervention is not helping to support him in any way. We need to be one family unit when handling this problem and his denial is sending the message that Jake's behaviour is okay with him. This recent evidence is now far too obvious for Brian to avoid seeing. He says that he now understands how his denial is hurting Jake, rather than supporting him, and agrees to be on board with our next move to repair the situation.

We decide that I will speak with Jake in private later in the day. I can see now that Brian's own childhood anguish is buried and in a protected place, so that he doesn't have to deal with his emotional pain. And these memories are triggered, coming to life whenever he hears me confronting or disciplining Jake. We cannot afford his squeamish discomfort to impair this opportunity to support Jake and prevent another possible catastrophe. We agree that Jake must be forced to remove the online game from his computer. It takes several hours to re-load the game, which Jake has obviously done overnight. The consequence, for Jake will be that he hands over his computer to us each night, so that he is not able to re-install or play the game. This rule will stand until he completes his final exams for this semester. Brian offers to speak with Nick about how the two of them cannot be party to enabling Jake, by ignoring that the dangers for him with this particular online game are very real.

Parenting is tough work, and we all want our kids to like us. Sometimes we let things go in order to maintain peace in the relationship. But in this particular case and many others where a voice of reason is needed, I take the attitude that Jake can hate me now, if he chooses, but I know it's necessary for me to be assertive in order to save him from himself. As a parent I can choose to do what is easy or I can choose to do what is right. And in this case, I fully grasp that it is right to intervene.

Jake understands clearly, before I even enter his hotel room. I had sent him a text earlier to say that we needed to speak in private, and he's had time to think about this. He knows that I am scared and that I am going to ask him to remove the game. He knows that I come from a place of love, and he understands that he cannot be left alone with the temptation of this draw, and that he can quite possibly drown in its deep waters, again. He takes responsibility in admitting that his previous behaviour is what has brought us to this place. He knows. He accepts. He removes the game while I sit with him. He is sad that it's come to this, again. And so am I. But he is in a much better place, both physically and emotionally, since the last time that we faced this. I caught it early, and as a result he has time to be clear about his motives; time to look at why the need to escape into this darker gaming world has reared its ugly head once again. He worked so hard this semester, and he remained focused, and he wanted the freedom to choose, and the freedom to reward himself. I understand. I tell him this, and I remind him that he can make healthier choices as a reward. This part we manage with more ease. And then I tell him that he must hand over his laptop to us each night until exams are done. Although Jake believes that he can shake the desire to re-install and play the game on his own, he knows that I will not sleep at night without this step, and he relents, for me. But I know that this is not going to be easy for him.

~~~~~~

The following day, Jake knocks on my hotel door to retrieve his laptop. He spends the morning with me, he in his corner of the room studying, while I sit and write at the desk. I make sure he's eating well and taking his remedies for ADD, to continue to help keep him healthy while he reviews his school notes.

We take a break mid-day and run an errand, and we stop at the house to see that the workers have finally returned, and the job site is busy again. The restoration continues to be a great source of frustration. While the insurance claim was tended to immediately, the work has been sluggish. We just want to go home, but there seems to be no rush on the restoration company's side. Any progress made now calls for a small celebration.

That evening Jake attends Writer's Ink with me at our local library. This program is offered to writers who wish to gather together, with their work, to share and receive feedback from each other. I only started attending myself, two weeks ago, and find it to be a great source of learning what may need to be revised in my literary work. Jake, who also loves to write, has decided that, while he's home from school, he'd like to attend. We both enjoy the evening, and I am quite impressed with Jake's work and with his input. He's an extremely intelligent young man, and I am fascinated by how he demonstrates his aptitude in a public forum. I also notice how much his body is shaking and twitching throughout the entire evening, and I wonder to myself why his system is quaking so dramatically. On the way home, I mention this to him, and he tells me that he was extremely nervous. How extraordinary that he could appear so relaxed and self-assured with his language, and yet his body was screaming FEAR! I express this, and he replies with, "Yes, I'm really good at hiding my emotions."

No kidding, I think to myself. That statement was far more revealing than I'm sure he intended it to be. He's expressing his honesty, to a fault. And I am left to think about all of the times that he has tried to lie to me, while his body language roared the truth.

Jake continues with his studying, we swim at the hotel pool when a break is needed, and every night he diligently hands over his laptop. We celebrate Nick's birthday in the city the night before Jake's first exam. He has assured me that he is prepared and taking the night off will be fine. I do believe him. Brian, Jake and I drive to the city and have a nice dinner at a restaurant with Nick, and then follow it up by trying out a new café in his neighbourhood for dessert. This particular place sets you up with refreshments and then with a flat fee one can enjoy a variety of video, card, or board games. We choose a board game called King of Tokyo, another strategy-based game that Jake always seems to win. We've joked and called him the Monopoly King for years, as he always amasses the greatest fortune of cash and equity every time we play. And this night is no different. Jake whips our butts and wins again. We have a great time, lots of interesting conversation and laughter, and we eventually make our way back to Nick's place to say our good-byes. We return to the hotel; another fabulous time spent together as a family.

For the next three days Jake and I are in Guelph so that he can write the first four of his five exams. I spend my time finishing Christmas shopping, have a visit with one of my cousins, spend some time with Iris, and do some writing at the coffee shop. Jake feels super confident after completing a couple of his finals, and he is fairly certain he passed. They are the two courses that have given him, and the majority of the other students, the biggest challenge. Data Structures and Micro Computing both sounds very dry to me, and something I would have no chance at understanding, so kudos to Jake for being able to tackle such challenging course material this semester.

The following week, Jake continues to study and prepare for the last exam. He decides to do some artwork design on his computer to fill in the empty spaces of time when he's not studying. This activity is a much more beneficial form of relaxation, and one that always builds his confidence in his own ability. He continues to do some writing, and his appetite for food is insatiable. I do my best to keep him well fed. And when we need a break to do something physical, we head to the hotel pool. Spending time in the water has been such a gift for all of us, but especially for Jake, who loves to swim.

Exam five is written and complete. And I exhale.

Chapter 39

It's now mid-December and Jake is officially finished semester one of year two in Software Engineering.

Only five more semesters to go, I say to myself. One day at a time, one semester at a time, and eventually Jake will have his degree. And my hope is that as Jake reaches each semester's end, and he personally grows and matures, that managing this particular educational system will get a little easier for him.

I look back and see that for Jake, nursery school was a hardship, elementary school was an enormous struggle, and middle school must have felt tortuous and lonely, ending in an extensive illness. And then secondary school was a challenge, with Jake catching up on credits after a missed first year. But eventually, with much support, Jake persevered with education and somehow found unconventional ways to succeed. Perhaps it is during the struggle and the lowest points that Jake is able to fully expand his ability, and fight for what is necessary in reaching his goals. I hope his learning doesn't always have to come through struggle.

In the meantime, I am full of congratulations for Jake. I am elated to see this day and this moment, and so is my son. I tell him that because I am providing both emotional and financial assistance, I insist on seeing his final grades for this semester. He agrees and tells me that they will be available in about two weeks. Although I believe that Jake is being honest about the work he's completed, there's still that tiny piece of me that needs to see some tangible proof.

~~~~~~

We celebrate a wonderful Christmas together. Our home is still not ready to return to, and so the insurance company provides us with more time in the hotel. By now, we have spent three months making this establishment our home away from home. I have Christmas cards hanging on the slats of the window blind, there's a Poinsettia on the desk beside a Christmas cookie tin that plays music. The gifts are all wrapped and there's food in the fridge in our little kitchenette to get us through the next few days. Nick and Jake share a comfortable room down the hall from us. Each of the hotel staff has made us feel welcome from day one, and they are aware that we will be celebrating the occasion alongside them. This setting is not ideal or traditional for Christmas celebrations, but we've learned to be adaptable and not waste a lot of energy on complaining. As we have done in the past, in a crisis we just improvise. It builds resilience and character in each one of us.

Nick arrives at the hotel Christmas Eve, mid-day, and we all get dressed up and attend an open house near our neighbourhood with friends, Derek and Lynn. Like so many of our friends, they have included us in some of their activities since we were evacuated from our home, and we're so grateful for their friendship. We have a couple of drinks; we eat, talk, laugh, and even play a game of billiards before we leave to go back to the hotel, wishing everyone a very Merry Christmas. We have a quick dinner in our hotel room and then we're off to see a movie playing at a cinema just out of town. When we return, Brian and I arrange our room and the gifts in a most festive manner, using a small table and the Poinsettia to make up for the fact that we don't have a Christmas tree. We're all adults, and we have no qualms about this. The space around us is not as important as the space we create between us and being together is what matters most.

Christmas Day arrives and our plans to open gifts before breakfast are quickly adjusted when we realize we've slept in until 9:30 a.m. Breakfast service in the hotel ends at 10:00 a.m. We send a text to Nick and Jake asking them to meet us downstairs. Surprisingly, the breakfast bar is filled with couples and families also celebrating the holidays, so it feels a lot less isolating than I had anticipated. We are all strangers, and yet we are all kin to the meaning of Christmas, and everyone is in a good mood, making our morning meal feel quite festive.

Later, we exchange gifts, with which we all seem quite satisfied. We agree that a family gift we received from our good friends, Cindy and Glen, is our absolute favourite; it's a wooden carved game board for Dice Poker, complete with dice and poker chips. We spend an hour swimming in the hotel pool, and then we all get dressed for dinner. But before we leave to eat, we decide to try a few rounds of this new game. None of us can resist the opportunity to play, and it turns out to be loads of fun! It's difficult to leave this entertainment, but we have Christmas dinner reservations and have to pick up Brian's mom. So, off we drive to Etobicoke.

Mom is in a great mood, and so elated to see her family. At 101 years young, she's managing quite well living on her own, but her advanced age is affecting her cognitive functions. Today, she can't remember Nick's and Jake's names, or which one of them is still attending school, and which of them is living in the city and working. This lapse in her memory is a new development, and we are very aware that her health may be a little fragile, now. She's a bit wobbly on her feet, at first, and needs a cane to maneuver herself. We get her to the car, and then we're off to the Marriott Hotel for dinner. The restaurant is full and bustling with diners at the buffet. We make our way to our table, order drinks, and then we're all off to retrieve a feast of beef, lamb, turkey, and all the trimmings.

I help mom with her meal and get her safely seated. We have a lovely time, and then we're back to mom's apartment to say good-bye for the night. Back at the hotel we all agree that more time needs to be made for playing Dice Poker, and a lot more laughter surfaces before we call it a night.

Boxing Day is spent playing and swimming, before I bring Nick back to the city. It's been a fabulous three days for all of us, and despite the fact that we didn't have a traditional Christmas in our home, we've had a holiday time that seemed more special than any other in years previous. Perhaps it's because of the togetherness required when in tight quarters, or a renewed appreciation for each other we've discovered through Brian's recent surgery, Jake's struggles with school, the flood and restoration ordeal, or all of it combined. Whatever it is, it's left a warm and bubbly feeling within each of us.

The following day is the best news day. I ask Jake if he thinks his final marks for semester one might be available. He replies with, "Let me go online and see right now."

We're both excited to see his results, and it's a fantastic feeling when they appear on his laptop's screen. He has passed all five credit courses! He has exceeded the grades he had anticipated getting in three of the courses. I am so happy for him, and so hugely relieved. He's done it, surpassing all expectations, and meeting all of the challenges.

"Congratulations Jake. Does this now give you confidence for the semesters to come?" I ask.

"No. What this actually means to me is that you finally have proof that I was doing the work that I said I was doing." Jake replies.

He continues "I knew how hard I was working, but dad always said that it would take some kind of written proof to erase the damage that had been done in my past, and now here it is."

For Jake it wasn't just a matter of working really hard and

meeting the course requirements. He knew that no matter how diligent he was about school, there would always be doubt in our minds. There would always be a trust factor that we all had to get past, and he finally had evidence of his commitment. This kind of success could only happen as a result of Jake's deep desire to overcome his struggles and work harder than ever to stay focused on school and on his personal goal of getting a degree. Our family could provide him all of the support he needed, but if staying in school was really not something that Jake wanted, then that deep chasm of frustration and apathy would be waiting to drag him down again.

I've often come to the understanding that school hasn't ever been a good fit for Jake. That didn't mean that I couldn't find a way to make it work somehow for him. University has been no exception. Year one and two were an absolute battle for Jake, and it required support from every possible direction to eventually pull him out from under himself. Monitoring closely, acting on my gut instincts, and insisting on exercising my parental authority and guidance, to ensure that Jake's adult education path continued with more ease was something I hadn't realized as a necessity until it was almost too late. Becoming eighteen is seen as such an important milestone in terms of growing up, and Jake's outward expression of wanting to be independent and "grown-up" threw a wrench into the mix. I let go way too soon. In my attempt to transition from parenting my child to parenting my adult child in a way that I believed would please Jake, I nearly lost him. Today, I celebrate not only Jake's success with his first semester, but also his ability to get honest with himself, with his journey to overcome his own internal battles, and his desire to grow into the man he wishes to be. There is room for trust again.

Chapter 40

During the course of this past year, I would often share my parenting experience with others in hopes of being a voice for those who were suffering in silence, and to start a very necessary conversation. I sensed that other mothers and fathers had to be struggling with some of these same issues, and I wanted to know how they were managing, or not. I was also looking for some of the support I needed to keep me going with this enormous task. I heard so many stories of parents, especially mothers, who felt the same frustrations, the same concerns, and who were so grateful to be able to share with me. There were stories of heartbreak, failure, and estrangement. Sadly, there were people who knew of a family whose child took their own life. But there were also encouraging stories of great achievement.

Many other parents were fully on board with my parenting methodology; taking Jake to counselling and to fitness classes, changing his diet, adding herbal remedies to his daily regime, and driving him back and forth to school, or removing him from school entirely. They understood the concept that parenting changes with a child's adulthood, and that it's a different and unique experience for each family. We don't share it with each other enough, and instead we suffer and stumble along in silence. Some well-meaning folks would tell me to medicate my son, or to consider removing Jake from university altogether. I would, at times, hear the statement,

"Maybe university isn't for Jake." And of course, there were desperate and trying times when I considered both of these options. Jake and I looked at and discussed the many choices. And I would ask him often if getting a degree was what he wanted. His answer was always the same; it was a definitive yes. My personal opinion, right from the start of Jake's education experience, was that just because the school curriculum and programming wasn't set up in a way that Jake could navigate with ease, it didn't mean he didn't deserve to be there and get an education that would advance his future goals. My feeling is that if you can't go up, then you just have to go around or through; you find a way to work through challenges.

For many students, living in residence or in a rental complex with other students, brings them their ideal sense of freedom, and gives them an opportunity to share and socialize with roommates. For Jake, a place of solitude and the supervision and care of an adult, be it myself or Iris, is a much better environment for him to stay focused on school, at this time.

For a lot of students, having any involvement by their parents while at university would be mortifying. And being seen at the counselling center might fill another young person with shame. Thankfully, Jake isn't one of those people. He eventually latched onto what he saw as a life raft in me and in the school's student services and used that to get himself back in the game when no other options were working. As a result, he was able to find his way, and learn how to be independent with as much support as was available. There is grace in humility and in honesty, and no shame should ever be attached to getting lost while looking to find one's way. And there is always a way. I believe that is the lesson Jake taught me and everyone who has been privy to his journey.

I hope my story reaches other parents who are embarking on this post-secondary experience with their child, or who may be in the midst of it already. Start a conversation with other parents, listen and learn. In sharing, I hope that you find a way, not necessarily my way, but a way to reach out and open a dialogue with your son or daughter and help to ease their discomfort or struggles in early adulthood. Keep your eyes and ears wide open and trust your intuition. Don't be afraid to impose your authority, as needed.

Although I wished I'd known sooner, I am now aware of who is at risk for depression, anxiety, and addiction, and what signs I could have looked for that indicated that Jake was struggling. I also wish I'd realized how some of my behavior, as a parent, wasn't modelling what I was trying to convey, as I was raising Nick and Jake. I had told both my sons that I would always have their backs, that they could call me at any time, day or night, if they were in need of help. I even said that they could call if they were in any kind of legal trouble. And I meant it. However, I also voiced, often that I had no tolerance for lying. This left Jake, in particular, very confused about opening up to me. While he wanted so desperately to figure out a solution on his own, he felt it necessary to lie to me and not draw any attention to the fact that there was a problem.

We, as parents have been taught to tell our children not to speak with strangers from the time they are very young. We also ask that they keep family issues close to home and not discuss personal conflict and affairs with anyone outside of our immediate family. I grew up with the expression that "we just don't air our dirty laundry with others". And then we wonder why our adult kids don't seek the help of a counsellor when they are having emotional difficulties while away at school. We inadvertently attach a sense of shame to the idea of sharing one's innermost feelings with someone who is not family. This is a great dis-service to our children. In retrospect, I would have encouraged counselling and given permission to Nick and Jake to seek help, if they ever needed it, before I launched them off to university.

My children grew up in an environment where my husband and I modelled independence, while also showing the importance of lending a hand to others in need. I am a health practitioner; clients come to me for support and guidance. My husband didn't like to ask for the service of others, and instead would read and study the how-to for fixing anything that needed repair in our home. He grew up in a family that taught him to be wary and untrusting of others, and then without realizing it, he passed this message along to our sons. We encouraged the boys to do volunteer work, and during the holiday season we would take them to soup kitchens to work alongside us on Christmas Day. This was normal for them, and although it taught them the value of kindness, it also gave them a false sense of security. How can one ask for help, when one has learned that they are the helper?

I see now, so very clearly that some of our communication was very confusing. In hindsight, I would have paid more attention to giving my sons the skills to recognize when they were struggling, and the freedom and permission to share their needs, and ask for help. There is great importance in teaching the lesson that requiring the aid of others is not a sign of weakness, but rather one of great strength.

Telling one's child not to be afraid of failing or asking for help and seeking counsel, at any age, is vital to their well-being. There is a great deal of learning through failure. It provides one the clarity to seek a solution and another path that may be more suitable. This experience can provide an environment for personal growth. There is no shame in feeling sadness, anxiety, and frustration. Just as we celebrate and reward our good feelings, it is equally as important to acknowledge our negative ones. They are a gift; they are there to show us that a shift is needed, that we've veered off the path. Anxiety, depression, and learning disabilities are far more common than you believe. Your child is not alone. Recognize that there is much support within your university and within your community, and that it's okay to be different. It's also okay to need assistance in the process when one has a learning disability or mental illness to contend with. It truly does take a village to raise a young child, but that same village may also be needed to continue to nurture the adult child.

The New Year will find us moving back into our newly restored home, and Jake will return to university for semester two. Of course, I will continue to keep my eyes and ears open to any indication that Jake may need my assistance, and I will, once again, offer him a support to lean on. As I have done in the past, I will dig deep and improvise to guide Jake in finding whatever works in overcoming any obstacles that may appear. My intention in the days to come is that I will get Jake through to the end by finding a way, one that is the best fit for him. It may not be conventional, but it's what I have to offer.

It's a new age, and I'm not my mother or my father. As has been necessary, I'm making it up as I go. There really are no hard rules to follow, and the goal is the same - to be a soft place for my son to land, to catch him when he falls, to help guide him in a meaningful direction, and eventually to launch him into the rest of his life a healthy, happy, and successful young man. I'm not doing what might be a good fit for other families. I am doing what is right for mine.

In my parenting experience, so far, I've written many new chapters; ones that don't resemble much of my own childhood at all. My children will take this and build on it, make changes of their own, and create their own personal version of the story, if and when they become parents.

In the meantime, my parenting chronicle continues.

Epilogue - Two Years Later

The flood restoration of our home takes another three months to complete before we are able move back in. We are elated. Home, sweet, home! Everything feels so fresh, and most importantly, spacious. Living for six months in a hotel room, while my husband recovers from major surgery and while we live with Jake's video gaming addiction struggle has been one of the greatest challenges for our family, ever. Coupled with this is the ongoing health struggles with both Brian and I's aging mothers. It is literally just one month later that social services and their doctors deem both requiring full care. Brian arranges to have his mother placed into a nursing home here in Ontario, while arrangements are made for my mother to move to residential care in British Columbia. We both do our best to comfort each other in having to agree to a decision that leaves us feeling guilty of letting our mothers down. It doesn't feel good, even though we understand, intellectually that it's the best decision for their personal safety. No one wants this living arrangement for their declining parent, yet it is a decision that many of us must face in time.

Jake continues to battle with anxiety at school and, of course, I worry. He eventually decides to check back in with the university therapist to arrange for regularly scheduled visits. Together, they come up with some strategies for handling his stress and worry. While Jake appears to be staying on top of his curriculum work, I am never certain if he is actually managing to do so. Year three has been incredibly tough and the workload is demanding. I am so grateful that Jake is living with Iris and not isolated once again in one of the school's residences. However,

I sense that he is still gaming for some of the time, while trying to maintain his academic standing. The same familiar feeling of trouble stirs inside of me. I can't fully control what Jake is doing while he is living in Guelph. I can only hope he's making smart decisions. I am now asking to see his final grades at the end of each semester. In April, Jake completes his school year and moves in with his brother, Nick, once again, and works at the software company in Toronto.

I spend part of the summer attending to the contents of my mother's home in British Columbia, on the far side of Canada (far removed from the home I have missed during the months of restoration), while Brian clears his mom's longtime apartment here in Ontario. This work is both emotionally taxing and physically draining as we re-visit each of their personal belongings and treasures and decide their fate. Thankfully, Jake is living with his brother and his level of care and supervision is reduced considerably for me.

Jake has another successful summer of employment and prepares to return to school for fourth year. He is still struggling to give up video gaming entirely but is somehow functioning and managing to fulfill his responsibilities at work. By this time, we learn that Iris has become ill and is unable to host Jake for the upcoming school year. So, Jake chooses to move into residence again at the university. While living with Iris wasn't perfect, and Jake did have set-backs and relapses with gaming, having Jake live in residence once more brings back all the terror I experienced during year two. On the day I move him into residence and set up his room, we both talk about how nervous we each feel, but with more time and small successes under Jake's belt, we are also hopeful and optimistic. We agree that he should remain in residence during weekdays, and return home on weekends, to continue to be monitored. Jake doesn't yet trust himself to be alone and struggles to self-regulate. I think deep down inside he understands, also, that video gaming interferes with school and his future success, but he's not ready to say that he will never, ever game again. He continues to believe that if he can manage his anxiety and depression, then he can still play video games, sometimes. I seem to be the only one that recognizes it as an addiction. I still see the anxiety and moodiness, the tremors, the edginess in Jake, and he gets quite agitated during any discussions about the idea of quitting gaming entirely. But I am also witnessing a young man who is determined to work hard and complete his degree program.

Jake joins and participates in a software organization at school and begins to make friends within the group. It's not easy to grow and nurture these friendships while he returns to our home every weekend, but it is a good step towards replacing the online friends he misses. First semester seems a little more manageable. However, not long after Jake begins, we receive news that our beloved family friend, Iris has suddenly passed. It is another painful blow for our family, and Jake doesn't take the news well. My heart breaks for Iris's remaining four daughters, who now face the agonizing journey ahead of living without their beautiful mother, just sixteen months following the loss of their sister, Barb. I feel like we are all still grieving deeply for Barb and accepting the loss of her mother is an impossible task for any of us to even consider. How much more pain can any of us endure? And, of course, I worry again about Jake's mental state back at school. I cannot take my foot off the gas, so to speak. It is a full-time job to monitor and support Jake, while also trying hard to remain somewhat distant, giving him the space he needs to be an adult. I feel exhausted much of the time, but I plow onwards. I have a responsibility, still, as his parent.

When winter comes, and daylight is reduced, Jake begins to battle deeper feelings of depression. This has been a pattern I have noted since university began four years ago. I increase his vitamin D intake and I encourage him to exercise more. Jake spends the winter snowboarding almost every weekend and he continues to join me in early morning fitness classes on Saturdays and Mondays. This seems to help. During this time, my husband and I, after many lengthy discussions, realize that it's time to sell our large country property and downsize. We had considered many different options over the past few years, and we finally conclude that Guelph would be the best place to move. Driving back and forth these past few years and visiting the community Iris had lived in, we came to see that it would offer us all that we needed for the empty nest years ahead. So, we busy ourselves in purging our home's contents to a feasible size and prepare to sell our home. This creates a distraction from watching Jake, and so I must let go, a little, and rely on blind faith for some of this time.

Jake completes year four, with a few hiccups and panicky moments, and moves back in with Nick for his last summer. His gaming relapses now come with less intensity, they're easier to recognize, and our family can steer Jake back on course with sobriety much quicker. Even though Jake's spiral of addiction comes in more manageable waves, I still just want them to completely stop! He begins to work, his third summer with the same software company. Brian and I spend this time moving into and renovating our new home in Guelph. I am quite distracted from Jake and assume that while in his brother's care he is in good hands. While Nick is still someone who enjoys playing video games, he is also aware of Jake's struggles with regulating his own gaming. There are times they still play, occasionally together. Nick feels that this creates a controlled environment. I disagree and feel it is a tease and a trigger for Jake. But again, they are two adults, and I must let go and trust that Jake will eventually see the addiction issue. The decision to quit, for good, must come from him. I have been able to force rules and consequences under my roof, but he is now living with his brother. I let go and focus on creating a new home in a new city. Jake will be able to live with us for this fifth and final year of school, and my rules will be implemented once again. Maybe this time, he will finally come to terms, fully with his addiction.

Partway through the summer, on a visit to Toronto with Jake, he announces to me that he decided to fully detox from video gaming for 90 days to see how he would feel. At this point he has successfully detoxed for 30 days. He seems quite proud. I am happy to hear this, but, of course there is a part of me that doesn't trust it will last. Jake still believes that he will one day be able to game again, without issues. I don't ask how he came to this decision, I just play along and tell him that I am happy to hear this news and I wish him much success. But deep down inside, I feel happy and hopeful for Jake's forward movement towards change.

Year five in school looks much different than any other year. With Jake now living with my husband and I in Guelph, Jake has the freedom to be with his friends from school on the weekends. He can join more clubs and activities that take place weeknights and weekends. Jake decides to tutor other students to make a little extra pocket money. He also joins the table tennis team, and together with some of his friends, he joins a dance group and martial arts classes. Jake marks ninety days of gaming detox and feels a sense of pride. He decides to continue this momentum of sobriety. I am now witnessing a more determined young man. However, in his drive to stop himself from video gaming, Jake becomes overly busy with a flurry of activities which now appear to be the new addiction. I fear burnout will occur if Jake continues with this ambitious schedule. I realize that he is running scared and filling up all of his time, so that he is not tempted to play video games. But he seems frazzled in trying to keep up. By early December Jake comes to the same conclusion. He realizes that he is exhausted. He now needs to create more balance. He takes the Christmas school break to rest and relax and continues to resist playing any video games. This is impressive!

Second semester comes as Jake continues to nurture and grow some great friendships at school and I no longer hear him talk about online friends of the past - ever. He spends less time running scared with a too-full activity schedule, and I see how much happier he appears. He completes his year at school and his degree program is done! It is a time to celebrate for more than one reason. Jake is now also a full nine months video gaming detoxed. He is determined to continue this path, and says he realizes that he cannot play a video game, ever again. He admits to his addiction - absolutely. He has a full life, with tangible friends, a full-time job to begin with a software company with a staff he loves, and he is looking forward to moving to Toronto permanently. I celebrate along with him. This is the best news, thus far! I now feel like I can breathe a little better, but I am still cautious. I don't know if the terror of Jake returning to his addiction will ever fully leave me. It has been a long, difficult, and at times, painful journey to get here. I can only hope that Jake continues this new, healthier life path. By this time, Nick and his girlfriend, Nicole have moved to a new apartment together, and Jake will have to find his own living accommodations. This next step is a fearful one for both Jake and I. Is he ready? Is this a good time? What will this look like? Will I sleep at night ever again?

During this last year, I have begun to share my story of lived experience with a video gaming addicted son. I have created a one-hour talk called One More Level: Video Gaming Addiction. I am sharing my story in schools and at mental health forums, to create more awareness to help other families. In June of this year, the World Health Organization established this addiction as an official Disorder. I am very happy about this news as it will aid in proper diagnosis and in creating more research to help with understanding and treatment for those with Video Gaming

Disorder. In researching information and preparing my talks, I learn so much more and I understand better why gaming is such an enormous draw. I now see how it can turn into an addiction for some, and why it is so important for parents to help their child with regulation and balance when using technology. I recently learned something of great value about Jake's journey into his recovery during a question and answer period, following one of my talks. I was presented with a question from a parent that I wasn't exactly sure how to answer. It was an excellent question and I did my best to give an explanation I thought may be close to the truth.

The question was, "Like the straw that broke the camel's back, what was the defining moment that made your son finally agree to fully detox from video gaming?" I answered that it was likely something that my son's older brother had said or done. He was a good influence and they were living together when Jake finally acknowledged that he had an addiction to video gaming. I also suggested that perhaps he realized that his future with the company he was working for hinged on him finally quitting playing video games. I then made a mental note to ask Jake this same question, so I wouldn't be caught off guard again with this query.

The next morning, I sent a text to Jake explaining what had transpired during my talk and queried him on what his defining moment actually was. His reply was, "Oh that's an easy one, it was at Nick's apartment that summer. I had another relapse for a short time during the summer, but in terms of what really hit me and pushed me to change, it was Nick getting angry at me, well and truly angry, when he came home to find me playing a multiplayer online game. What upset him was that I chose a time when I knew he would be out for the night to play (he came home unexpectedly), showing that it was, to me, still something I was trying to hide, and thus didn't understand my own addiction problems. What broke me was when he then explained how he looked at me, what he thought of me, and who I was to him – all the good stuff. It was a counter to all my own internal self-esteem problems and the validation I'd been looking for from him. He then took me to the mirror by the back door beside the kitchen and made me look at myself. He made me say 'I'm a success.' It was one of the hardest things I've ever done. It took me a long time staring at that mirror with him silently beside me. Then he held me as I cried and let me crawl into bed with him and continue crying while holding onto him. That was the point where I went from "I don't have a problem" to "I have an addiction" in my head. Or rather, "gaming isn't the problem" to "I have an addiction."

Reading this filled my heart with such love for both of my sons, as I could feel the intense pain of that moment they had both experienced. Jake says he still tears up every time he thinks about it. I do recall the day after this moment between my two sons occurred. But I had no idea of its magnitude at that time. I was visiting Nick the next morning, and he told me that he'd caught Jake gaming again and finally gave him a piece of his mind. He said that Jake was very upset, but he didn't provide any more details. As he was speaking I could see into his bedroom and commented that his pillow looked very wet. I asked if he was feeling well and did he have a fever last night. He said no he wasn't sick, and that although he had gotten angry with Jake, he wasn't a cold-hearted person. He let Jake sleep with him and consoled him through his tears, afterwards.

I also recall the day that Jake told me that he had been fully detoxed from gaming for thirty days, during that summer, and was committed to a ninety-day detox to see how he'd feel. He didn't mention the blowup between he and his brother, and I acted as though I knew nothing about it. After more than two years of struggling and supporting Jake through many relapses, I was so pleased that he'd stopped denying his addiction and was finally facing it, head on. I was distracted with moving to Guelph, and I was feeling so desperate for Jake to face the inevitable, that I don't really think it mattered much to me as to why Jake came to terms with his addiction. I was just grateful that he did.

I am not at all surprised that it was Jake's older brother, Nick who saved the day - perhaps even a lifetime. He's been the best brother since the day that Jake was born. He has always cared for and loved Jake, unlike any other siblings I've ever witnessed or heard of. They have had and still have an amazing bond. Nick finally fully understood that Jake had an addiction to gaming, and he was willing to do whatever it took to get him to recognize it. And he succeeded. Today, Jake is fourteen months gaming-free.

Quitting gaming is possible; making the decision to do so is the biggest hurdle for a gaming addict. I'm not going to say that detox is easy. Jake would agree. It is literally a one-day-at-a-time process that requires intense commitment, mindfulness, and hard work. It also takes enormous support from the addict's family.

Mid-summer of this year we lost the Uskoski matriarch. My husband's mother passed away, peacefully just thirteen days shy of her 104th birthday. And while we acknowledge that losing one's remaining parent is sad, hers was a life to be celebrated. She lived life well and long. In contrast, I am mourning the loss of the mother I once knew, as Dementia is robbing my own mother of her cognitive function at just age seventy-seven.

Jake moved to Toronto two months after he began working full time. He found the long commute from Guelph to Toronto far too long. He admitted he wasn't ready to live on his own, but he knew he wanted to live in Toronto. He chose to move in with his dear friend he'd known since kindergarten, and his friend's girlfriend; two decent and wonderful individuals. They both know his story and Jake felt they would be a good influence on him. The move, of course, was scary for me, but I didn't want that to impede with Jake's ability to move forward. Jake, himself understood this, and conscientiously made the decision to keep me abreast of his movements, as much as possible until I felt comfortable. With a full year of no video gaming at all in Jake's life, I felt he had a very good chance of creating success for himself with this move. I supported him fully and appreciated that he was aware of needing to help me find comfort in his parting by staying in constant contact.

Jake is doing well and finding his way, living in Toronto, on his terms. We are still in close contact. Recently, I received the following text from Jake:

"I've been living in the city for 2 months now and... I haven't crashed. I haven't hit crisis. I've had ups and downs, but I'm finding routine.

Mom, I'm... I'm okay. It just dawned on me that I'm okay. I'm legitimately, realistically, happily okay.

I was so scared I wouldn't be okay. I was horrified I'd fail, or I'd relapse. I was so terrified I would be unable to take care of myself.

I've found a lovely sandwich shop that makes good, healthy food (he still hates cooking). I have friends I see and hang out with. I do laundry. I fold laundry. I vacuum. I take out the trash. I take time to relax and watch TV or play card games with my roommates. I'm working on my personal projects. I'm physically active. I'm happy at work. I'm happy at home."

Words are such a gift, and there are no words I have ever wanted to hear more in these past few years. The greatest lesson I have learned from this experience is to never give up on your child. Never give up on your addicted child. Regardless of age, our children need to always know that we, as their parent will always be their safe place to land, their greatest support system, and their biggest cheerleaders.

Today marks the first time in twenty-three years that I do not have a child entering into a school system. My two sons have graduated, have full-time jobs, and are living away from home. It has been a long and difficult journey, at times, but we have reached the pinnacle of full independence.

Is my job as a parent now done? No. There are always teachable moments, even into the adult years. And I am still Mom. I will still care for and have concerns for both of my sons. And I will be here, as they need me.

But for the first time in a very long time, as mom, I feel that I can finally exhale.

ABOUT THE AUTHOR

Elaine Uskoski is an Author, Speaker, Holistic Health Practitioner and the mother of two adult sons.

She now shares her personal experience with her youngest son, speaking in schools and mental health forums about video gaming addiction, to create awareness and prevention.

Elaine lives in Guelph, Ontario, Canada with her husband.

www.ElaineUskoski.com